U0084981

編輯小語

　　面對國外客戶，您會緊張，辭不達意嗎？想不想擁有一口流利的英語，成為縱橫商場的生意尖兵？

　　學習關心您的需求，特別將您和老外談生意時，可能碰到的情況一網打盡，彙編成「客戶接待英文」（*Spoken Business English*）。內容從迎接客戶開始，教您如何招待客戶，推銷產品，陪客戶參觀工廠，解決糾紛，順利簽約，完成交易。您到國外出差，事先定機位、旅館，途中需要處理突發事件，本書都為您設想周全，面面顧到。您只要依樣畫葫蘆，便足以應付自如。

　　「客戶接待英文」分為三十課，把你必備的商業知識濃縮成為生動逼真、好學好用的四組**對話範例**（*Model Dialogs*）和**補充對話**（*Supplementary Dialogs*），提供您最實用的商業術語與字彙，讓您現學現用，事半功倍。

　　此外，每課課後均附上一篇**經驗談**（*Business Advice*），告訴您貿易實務的常識及歐美國情，基本禮儀，提醒您不可輕忽的小節，讓您成為博聞多禮，潛力無限的經理人才。

　　忙！? 如何突破瓶頸，追求卓越？善用零碎時間，閱讀「客戶接待英文」（*Spoken Business English*），一天一課，三十天輕鬆完成充電，使您信心洋溢，樂在工作 **!!**

編者　謹識

CONTENTS

Part 3　Nearing an Agreement
／ 契約將成

Part 4　Entertaining a Buyer
／ 接待買主

Part 5 Going Overseas ／ 海外出差

PART 1

Initial Contact

第一次接觸

LESSON 1

Picking up a Buyer

MODEL DIALOGS

1

A : Excuse me, but are you Mr. Johnson of City Bank?

B : Yes, I am.

A : How do you do? I'm David Wang of Acer Industrial Corp..

B : How do you do? Glad to meet you.

A : Did you *have a good flight*?

B : Yes, it was enjoyable, thanks.

A : That's good to hear.

---

pick up 接

Corp. = corporation 〔͵kɔrpə'reʃən〕 *n.* 公司

第一課

接買主

對話範例

1

A：抱歉，請問您是花旗銀行的強森先生嗎？

B：是的，我是。

A：你好！我是宏碁電腦的王大衞。

B：你好！很高興認識你。

A：飛機旅行還愉快吧？

B：對呀，相當愉快，謝謝。

A：聽到你這樣說真好。

---

have a good flight 飛機旅行愉快

2

A : Welcome to Taiwan, Mr. Brown.

B : Nice to meet you, Mr. Wang.

A : I've been *looking forward to* meeting you, too.

B : Thank you very much for coming to meet me.

A : No trouble at all. Let me take your things.

B : Oh, that's all right. They're not heavy.

3

A : (*Calling out in the crowd*) Here I am, Mr. Harris.

B : Hi, Mr. Lin. How are you?

A : Fine, thanks. It's nice to see you again.

B : It's been quite a while, hasn't it?

A : Right. It's been almost 3 years since I saw you in Los Angeles.

B : You haven't changed a bit.

A : Thank you. Neither have you.

---

change〔tʃendʒ〕*v.* 改變
look forward to 盼望

2

A：歡迎到台灣來，布朗先生。

B：很高興認識你，王先生。

A：我也一直盼望認識你。

B：非常感謝你來接我。

A：一點也不麻煩。讓我替你拿行李。

B：喔，還好。行李不重。

3

A：（在人群中喊）我在這兒，哈瑞斯先生。

B：嗨，林先生。你好嗎？

A：很好，謝謝。很高興再見到你。

B：已經好些日子沒見面了，不是嗎？

A：是啊，打從上回我在洛杉磯見過你到現在，已經差不多要三年了。

B：你一點也沒變。

A：謝謝！你還不是一樣。

4

A : How was your flight?

B : Not bad. But I'm a little tired.

A : Have you made hotel reservations?

B : No, the trip was so sudden.

A : Well then, let me make some arrangements for you.

B : I'd appreciate that.

A : Shall I take you to a hotel now?

B : Yes, please.

SUPPLEMENTARY DIALOGS——

A : You must be tired after such a long flight.

B : Yes, I'm feeling a little *jet lag*.

A : I'm pleased to meet you, Mr. Smith.

B : The pleasure is mine.

A : Is this your first trip to Taiwan?

B : Yes, it is.

A : I've *booked a room* for you at the Hilton Hotel.
Single, for a week.

B : Oh, good. Thanks.

---

arrangement〔ə'rendʒmənt〕*n.* 安排

appreciate〔ə'priʃɪ,et〕*v.* 感激

reservations〔,rɛzə've ʃənz〕*n. pl.* （旅館房間的）預訂

4

A：您的飛機旅行如何？

B：還不壞。不過，我有點累。

A：你有沒有事先訂好旅館？

B：沒有，這趟旅行這麼匆促。

A：唔，那麼，讓我替你安排。

B：非常感激。

A：我現在載你去旅館，好嗎？

B：好的，謝謝。

補充會話

A：在如此長途飛行之後，您一定有些疲倦。

B：是呀，我覺得有些不適應時差。

A：很高興見到你，史密斯先生。

B：這是我的榮幸。

A：這是你第一次到台灣來嗎？

B：是的。

A：我已經在希爾頓訂了個房間。是單人房，可以住一星期。

B：喔，很好。謝謝！

---

jet lag 時差

book〔buk〕*v*. 訂位

BUSINESS ADVICE

到 機場迎接客戶,事先要和對方約在特定地點見面(如:機場的咖啡廳),免得找不到人。與人相約,要守時,讓客戶久等,是很失禮的行為。

如果彼此沒見過面,可先問清對方的外型、特徵和當天的穿著(如:對話範例1)。當天到達約定地點,發現有符合特徵的人,即可直接向前詢問。如:

A: Excuse me, are you Mrs. Adams?
(對不起,請問您是亞當太太嗎?)
B: Hello! It's a pleasure to meet you at last.
(哈囉!很高興終於見到你。)

在 機場迎接客戶、朋友的時候,可以使用下列簡單用語,來打招呼:

Did you have a good flight?
(你有個愉快的飛機旅行嗎?)

Did you have a nice trip?
(旅途愉快嗎?)

I hope you had a nice trip.
(我希望你有個愉快的旅行。)

I hope you have enjoyed your flight.
(我希望你對這越飛機旅行感到滿意。)

此外，在道別的時候，遣詞用字上，也有些微妙的差異。對初次見面的人，道別的時候，多使用 "**meet**"（認識）。如：

I've enjoyed meeting you.
I'm very glad to have met you.
（我很高興認識你。）

然而，對於認識的人，則使用 "**see**"（見到）這個動詞。如：

I'm very glad to have seen you.
（非常高興見到你。）

至 於我們常用的「慢走」、「好走」的客套話，西方人則用下面幾句慣用語代替。如：

Have a nice day!
Have a good time!
（祝你玩得開心！）

Had a nice day!
I hope you had a nice day.
（希望你玩得還算開心。）

在晚上道別的時候，與其說 "good-bye"，倒不如說

Good night!

LESSON 2

From the Airport to the Hotel

MODEL DIALOGS ————————

1

A : My name is David Wang. Here's my card.

B : I'll give you mine, too.

A : The company car is waiting outside. Shall we go?

B : OK. Is it going to be very far?

A : No, we'll get to the office *right away*. (*On opening a car door*) Please sit in the back seat.

B : Thank you.

———————————

card 〔kɑrd〕 *n.* 名片
right away 馬上

第二課
從機場到旅館

對話範例

1

A：我是王大衞。這是我的名片。

B：我也會給你我的名片。

A：公司的車子在外面等著。我們可以動身了嗎？

B：好的。路途會很遠嗎？

A：不，我們馬上就到辦公室。（打開車門時說）請坐後座。

B：謝謝。

2

A : (*In the car*) It's very warm, isn't it?

B : It sure is. How's business recently?

A : A little slow, I'm afraid, but we expect things to pick up soon.

B : That sounds encouraging.

A : How long will you be in Taipei?

B : My schedule is rather tight. I have to **leave for** Hong Kong on Thursday.

A : We'll have to hurry, in that case.

3

A : Yes? May I help you?

B : I'd like to **check in**, please.

A : Do you have a reservation?

B : Yes. My name is John Smith. I made it with the ABC Travel Agency in L.A..

A : No problem. I have the reservation here.

---

slow〔slo〕*adj.* 不景氣的

pick up 改善

leave for 前往

encouraging〔ɪnˈkɝdʒɪŋ〕*adj.* 給予希望的

2

A：（在車上）天氣很暖和，對不對？

B：的確是。最近生意如何？

A：恐怕，有點不景氣，但是我們期望情況很快有進展。

B：那聽起來還有希望。

A：你會在台北待多久？

B：我的時間表相當緊湊。星期四我得前往香港。

A：那樣的話，我們必須趕快。

3

A：呃，請問有什麼可以效勞的地方？

B：我想住宿。

A：有預訂房間嗎？

B：有。我的名字是約翰史密斯。洛杉磯的 ABC 旅行社替我辦的預約。

A：沒問題。這裏已經預約好了。

---

check in 投宿旅館

in that case 那樣的話

4

A : Here's your hotel. Let me help you with the formalities at the front desk.

B : You are very kind.

A : (*In a hotel room*) I think you'd like to unpack and
freshen up.

B : Yes. Just give me a minute to take a shower and
change my clothes.

A : *Take your time*. I'll be back around 6.

B : OK. I'll be ready by that time.

SUPPLEMENTARY DIALOGS———

A : Would you like me to show you around ?

B : Thanks. That's very kind of you.

A : How far is it to the office ?

B : It'll take about 40 minutes or so if the traffic isn't
too heavy.

A : How's the marketing these days ?

B : Pretty good. Sales have been up these days.

A : When should I pick you up ?

B : At 10 tomorrow morning, please.

---

formalities 〔 fɔr'mælətɪz 〕 *n. pl.* 手續
unpack 〔 ʌn'pæk 〕 *vt.* 打開行李

4

A：你的旅館到了。讓我幫你到前面櫃台辦理手續。

B：你眞好心。

A：（*在旅館房間*）我猜你想打開行李拿出衣物，然後輕鬆一下。

B：是呀，給我一點點時間，沖個涼，換一下衣服。

A：慢慢來。我大約六點左右回來。

B：好的。我會在那之前準備好。

補充會話 ──────────────

A：想不想讓我帶你四處看看？

B：謝謝。你眞好。

A：到辦公室有多遠？

B：如果交通不太擁擠的話，大概四十分鐘左右。

A：這些日子市場狀況如何？

B：相當好。這些日子銷售量已上揚。

A：我應該什麼時候來接你呢？

B：請明早十點來接我。

---

freshen up 盥洗打扮

take your time 慢慢地做

BUSINESS ADVICE

按照我們一般打招呼的習慣，握手的同時，往往會順手遞上名片。但是在歐美，人們只有在認為，有必要繼續連絡的時候，才會遞上名片。因此，和西方人士交往時，必須注意的一點就是，在我們遞出名片的同時，似乎就在強迫對方交換名片，這是很容易造成失禮的情況。一般而言，只有在告別的時候，在適當的時機中提出來，名片才能顯出它的意義和功效。以下是交換名片時，常用的句子：

Hello! I'm David Wang. Here's my business card.
（嗨！我是王大衛。這是我的名片。）

Oh, let me give you my business card before I forget.
（喔，趁我還沒忘記以前，讓我把名片給你。）

Well, it was nice to have met you. Here's my card. Please call me any time.
（哇，認識你真好。這是我的名片，你隨時可以打電話給我。）

其他時候，譬如說在由機場到市區的路上，如果能彼此多聊聊，是比較理想的。此時，不外是由天氣、彼此的近況作為話題，來打破僵局。這時，你可以說：

It's very warm, isn't it ?

（天氣很暖和，對不對？）

Did everything go all right ?

（一切都還好吧？）

How's your business ?

（生意如何？）

　　另外，如果在坐車中途，恰巧看到自己公司的招牌，便可以藉機介紹自己公司，同時拿這個題目打開話題。你可以這麼說：

Please look at that billboard. It's advertising our new product, SK-X.

（請看那個招牌。它在宣傳我們公司的新產品，SK-X。）

◉ 大風吹！猜猜看哪個才是你的座位？

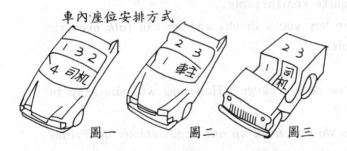

車內·座位安排方式

圖一　　　圖二　　　圖三

　　一號是指地位最高的人，四號是地位最低的人。在有司機的情況下（如圖一），後座右側是上座；如果是車主自己開車（如圖二），則車主旁邊的座位才是上座。但吉普車，卻有與一般轎車不同的座位安排，即使有司機，前座右側仍是上座（如圖三）。

LESSON 3

Meeting Arrangements

MODEL DIALOGS ─────────

1

A : Did you find your hotel comfortable?

B : Yes, quite comfortable.

A : Let me buy you a drink, and we can **talk over** the schedule.

B : O.K.

A : (*At the hotel lounge*) How long will you stay in Taipei?

B : I hope we can **wind up** our negotiations by Friday.

A : That would be sufficient time to complete them.

───────────

talk over 討論
lounge 〔 laundʒ 〕 *n.* 休息室
schedule 〔ˈskɛdʒul 〕 *n.* 時間表
wind up 結束

第三課
安排會面

對話範例 ————————————————

1

A：你覺得旅館還舒適吧？
B：對，相當舒適。
A：讓我請你喝杯飲料，然後我們可以討論時間表。
B：好啊。
A：（在旅館休息室）你會在台北待多久？
B：我希望在禮拜五之前，我們能夠結束談判。
A：那會有足夠的時間完成。

---

negotiation〔nɪ,goʃɪˈeʃən〕*n.* 談判
sufficient〔səˈfɪʃənt〕*adj.* 足夠的
complete〔kəmˈplit〕*vt.* 完成

2

A : Could you arrange a meeting with your boss?

B : Of course. I've arranged for your luncheon meeting with my boss.

A : Fine.

B : And here's your schedule for tomorrow.

A : Thank you.

B : You're welcome. You'll be spending most of it touring a factory. And you'll be having dinner with my manager in the evening.

3

A : (*In the office*) You have a nice office.

B : Thank you. Please come along. We can talk in the conference room.

A : All right.

B : Please have a seat and make yourself comfortable. My manager will be here soon.

A : I see.

B : Would you like coffee or something cold?

A : Coffee would be fine.

You're welcome. 不客氣。

luncheon〔'lʌntʃən〕 *n.* 午餐（較 lunch 正式）

tour〔 tʊr 〕 *v.* 視察

2

A：能安排和你的老闆見個面嗎？

B：當然可以。我已經安排你和老闆午餐會談。

A：很好。

B：還有，這是您明天的行程表。

A：謝謝。

B：不客氣。明天大部分時間你會視察工廠，然後和我們經理共進晚餐。

3

A：（在辦公室）你辦公室很舒適。

B：謝謝。請跟我來。我們可以在會議室談。

A：好的。

B：請坐，不要拘束。我們經理很快就過來。

A：知道了。

B：你要咖啡還是其他冷飲？

A：就咖啡好了。

---

conference room 會議室

have a seat 請坐

make oneself comfortable 不要拘束

4

A : Mr. Brown, this is Mr. Park, my manager.

B : How do you do, Mr. Brown? Welcome to our company.

C : How do you do? It was nice of you to send your man to the airport to meet me.

B : I'm sorry I couldn't meet you at the airport. Here's my card.

C : Here's mine, too.

B : First let's have some coffee, shall we?

C : Sounds like a good idea.

SUPPLEMENTARY DIALOGS——

A : Our company is situated on 11th floor. Please take the elevator over there.

B : I see.

A : I'm sorry to have kept you waiting.

B : That's all right.

A : May I offer you something to drink?

B : No, thanks.

A : How would you like your coffee?

B : Black, please.

---

elevator〔'ɛlə,vetɚ〕 *n.* 電梯

black coffee 純咖啡(不加牛奶、糖)

4

A：布朗先生，這是我們經理，派克先生。

B：布朗先生，你好嗎？歡迎到我們公司。

C：你好。你真體貼，派人到機場接我。

B：抱歉不能親自到機場接你。這是我的名片。

C：這是我的名片。

B：讓我們先用些咖啡，好嗎？

C：聽起來不錯。

補充會話

A：我們公司在11樓。請到那邊搭電梯。

B：知道了。

A：抱歉讓你久等。

B：沒關係。

A：你要什麼飲料？

B：不用了，謝謝。

A：您喜歡喝什麼咖啡？

B：純咖啡，謝謝。

BUSINESS ADVICE

在 西洋禮俗中，互相介紹的禮儀，有下面
幾項慣例：

a. 異性間相互介紹時，應先將男性介紹給女性。

b. 同性間相互介紹時，應將地位較低者介紹
給地位較高者，把未婚者介紹給已婚者。

c. 把年幼者介紹給年長者。

d. 同性間，當年紀、地位都相似的時候，則
先將和自己比較熟悉的人介紹給其他人。

禮 貌上，介紹者與被介紹者均應起立，但
異性間相互介紹的場合中，女性並無起
立的必要。不過，如果在座衆人之中，有地位
較高，或者是年紀較長的人，那麼女性也應該
起立，才合乎禮儀。

● FORGET ME NOT !

記住對方的姓名，是種禮貌。像How do you do, Mr. Brown？
How's going, Miss Lin？這類寒暄用語，由於加上了對方
的名字，而使聽話的人感到倍增親切。所以在介紹的時候，
一方面要注意聽對方的名字，一方面還要正確無誤地把對方
的名字背起來。萬一聽不清楚的時候，可以再請教對方一次，
總之，以儘可能不要叫錯對方名字爲原則。

看看下列情況，介紹人該怎麼說：

1. Miss Evans, may I introduce Mr. Smith?
（伊凡小姐，容我向妳介紹史密斯先生。）

2. Mrs. White, Miss Lee, this is Mr. Park.
（白太太，李小姐，這位是派克先生。）

3. Mrs. Brown, this is Mr. Smith；Mr. Harris, Mr. Smith.
（布朗太太，這位是史密斯先生；哈瑞斯先生，史密斯先生。）

4. Mrs. Jones, this is Mr. Lee and Mr. Harris.
（瓊斯太太，這位是李先生，還有哈瑞斯先生。）

Mr. Morgan, this is Mr. Lee and Mr. Harris.
（摩根先生，這是李先生，還有哈瑞斯先生。）

以下是被介紹者常用的語句，如：

- How do you do？ I'm very happy to meet you.
（你好，很高興認識你。）

- I'm very happy to make your acquaintance.
（很高興認識你。）

- I've heard so much about you.
（久仰大名。）

- I've been looking forward to this occasion.
（我一直期盼這個機會。）

LESSON 4

A Call from a Buyer

MODEL DIALOGS

1

A : (*On the phone*) When are you coming to Taipei ?

B : I'm arriving on April 8, Pan Am Flight 602. **It's due** at 10:30 a.m.

A : I'll be at the airport to meet you.

B : **I'd appreciate it**.

A : By the way, how will I recognize you ?

B : I'm about six feet seven. I have blond hair and wear glasses.

A : I see.

---

due〔dju〕 *adj.* 預期的

appreciate〔ə'priʃɪ‚et〕 *v.* 感激

第四課

買主來電

對話範例

1

A：（電話中）你什麼時候要來台北呢？
B：我四月八日會到，搭泛美六〇二號班機。預定當天上午十點半到達。
A：我會到機場接你。
B：非常感謝。
A：對了，我怎麼認得出你呢？
B：我大約六呎七吋，金髮碧眼，戴眼鏡。
A：知道了。

---

recognize〔ˈrɛkəgˌnaɪz〕*vt.* 認得
blond〔blɑnd〕*adj.* 金髮碧眼的

2

A : (*On the phone*) Export Department. May I help you ?

B : This is Bill Carson from Crown Cycle Ltd. We are thinking of buying some of your products through **OEM** business.

A : Oh, are you ? May I ask where you are now ?

B : I've just arrived at Chiang Kai-Shek International Airport.

A : I'll come there to pick you up.

B : That's very kind of you. **How long will it take** ?

A : Let's see... about half an hour or so.

B : I see. I'll be waiting for you at the coffee shop in the arrival lounge.

3

A : (*On the phone*) This is Mike. How are you ?

B : Fine, thank you, and you ?

A : Pretty good, thank you. How nice to hear your voice again.

B : Where are you calling from ?

A : From my hotel — Howard Plaza Hotel. How about having lunch at my hotel ?

B : That's great !

A : **What time shall we make it** ?

OEM 初級設備製造業 (*Original Equipment Manufacturing*)

2

A： （電話中）出口部。我能爲您效勞嗎？

B： 我是環冠有限公司的比爾卡森。我們打算透過初級設備製造業，買一些你們的產品。

A： 噢，是嗎？請問您現在在那裏？

B： 我剛抵達桃園中正國際機場。

A： 我會到那裏去接你。

B： 你真好心。要花多久時間呢？

A： 我想想……大概要半小時左右吧。

B： 知道了。我會在入境室的咖啡廳等你。

** OEM （初級設備製造業）從其他製造商那兒，買組件來裝配，藉以生產複雜、精密的設備（如：電腦系統）。

3

A： （電話中）我是邁克。你好嗎？

B： 很好，謝謝，那你呢？

A： 還不錯，謝謝你。很高興再聽見你的聲音。

B： 你在哪裏打的電話？

A： 從旅館——福華大飯店。到我住的旅館吃午飯如何？

B： 太棒了。

A： 我們約什麼時間好呢？

4

A : (*On the phone*) Hello, is this Taipei, 723—4567 ?

B : Yes, it is.

A : This is Chicago. We have *a collect call* for Mr. Park. Is Mr. Park there ?

B : Yes, he's here. I'll get him to come to the phone now.

C : Hello. This is Mr. Park speaking.

A : You have a call from Mr. Miller. Will you accept the charge ?

C : Yes, I will.

A : Thank you. Mr. Miller is *on the line*.

SUPPLEMENTARY DIALOGS———

A : May I speak to your Sales Manager, please ?

B : I'm sorry, but he's out of the office. Can I do anything for you ?

A : Mr. Park is on another line. Do you want to hold ?

B : No. I'll call back in five minutes.

A : Can you tell me the details over the phone ?

B : I'll tell you now. Would you note them down ?

A : I guess I should *hang up* now.

B : Well, thank you for calling.

---

collect call 對方付費電話
charge〔tʃɑrdʒ〕*n.* 費用
on the line 電話接通

4

A：（電話中）喂，是台北，723－4567嗎？

B：是的。

A：這裏是芝加哥。有一通派克先生的付費電話。派克先生在嗎？

B：在。我現在找他來接電話。

C：喂，我是派克先生。

A：有一通米勒先生打來的電話。你願意付費嗎？

C：好的。

A：謝謝。電話通了，可以和米勒先生說話了。

補充會話 ————————————————

A：請找你們的銷售經理，謝謝！

B：抱歉，他不在辦公室。我能爲你做什麼嗎？

A：派克先生在接另一通電話。您要繼續保持通話嗎？

B：不用了。我五分鐘後再打。

A：你能在電話裏告訴我細節嗎？

B：我現在告訴你。你願意記下來嗎？

A：我想我現在應該掛電話了。

B：謝謝你打電話來。

---

on another line 在（電話的）另一線

detail〔ˈditel, dɪˈtel〕*n.* 細節

hang up 掛斷電話

BUSINESS ADVICE

打 電話時，由於無法看到對方的容貌、表情，只能聽到對方的聲音，因此對於聲音的敏感度就格外重要。對於分派到出口部門的新進人員而言，第一件令人頭大的事，就是接到外國人打來的電話。

● Telephone Phobia—電話恐懼症？

有人從聽筒中一聽到 " Hello " 的聲音，恨不得能趁別人不注意的時候，偷偷地掛掉電話。尤其在與外國人通電話時，一方面聽不太懂，一方面又趕不上對方說話的速度，因而造成溝通不良的情況產生。若想克服恐懼感，首先，必須要把「聽不懂很丟臉」的念頭去掉才行。

　　當你趕不上說話者的速度時，可以婉轉地說：

I'm sorry I can't follow you. Would you repeat it ?
（抱歉，我跟不上你。你願意再說一次嗎？）

I couldn't catch you. Would you speak more slowly ?
（我跟不上你。你願意講慢一點嗎？）

　　一般而言，對方會應要求而放慢速度。

萬 一周遭環境太吵，以致於無法聽清楚對方說話時，如果您說的是：

Will you speak more clearly?
（你能不能講清楚點？）

自尊心強的老外聽來，可能會感到不高興，因為用 " clear " 這個字，意思是把聽不清楚變成了是由於老外的失誤造成的。建議不妨改用以下說法，較為合適：

Would you speak more loudly, please?
（你可以講大聲一點嗎？）

I can't hear you. Would you speak a little louder?
（我聽不見你說的話。你願意講大聲一點嗎？）

當 你忙得不可開交，卻接到一通很冗長的電話時，可以用

Thank you for calling.
（謝謝你打電話來。）

I wish we could talk longer, but I have kept my visitor waiting.
（我希望我們能多談一會兒，但我已經讓訪客久等了。）

之類的句子，來表示 " Good-bye " 的意思，使對方了解到談話應該結束，而不會顯得沒有禮貌。

LESSON 5

A New Business Contact

MODEL DIALOGS ——————

1

A : I'd like to show you some of our products.

B : Can you show me some catalogs first?

A : Here you are. I believe that they will allow you to lower costs.

B : Do these cover your complete product line?

A : Yes, everything we export is included.

B : May I look at some samples?

A : Sure. I'm very confident of the quality of our products.

——————————————————

catalog〔'kætḷ,ɔg〕 *n*. 貨物價目表

lower〔'loɚ〕 *v*. 減少

第五課
見新客戶

對話範例

1

A：我樂意向您展示我們一些產品。
B：能先給我貨物價目表嗎？
A：在這兒。我相信它們會讓你減少花費。
B：這些目錄包括你們所有產品系列嗎？
A：是的，我們所有出口的商品都包括其中。
B：我能看看樣本嗎？
A：當然，我對我們商品品質，非常有信心。

---

line〔lain〕*n.* 系列

2

A : Would you like a cigarette?

B : No, thank you. Go ahead.

A : Well, I understand you're rushed for time. So, what do you say to our **getting down to** some discussion?

B : No problem. I'm interested in your new model **passenger cars** advertised in this month's issue of the "CARS".

A : How many cars do you think you can buy?

B : About 200 to 300.

3

A : I'm finding a suitable agent to represent us.

B : You **produce** sneakers, don't you?

A : That's one of our products —we have quite a few other sporting goods.

B : I know. The demand for your brand is growing fast here.

A : I think you'd be just the people to work together with.

B : I'd be very happy to consider doing so.

---

get down to 靜下心來工作
passenger car 客車
represent〔ˌrɛprɪˈzɛnt〕*vt.* 代表
brand〔brænd〕*n.* 品牌;商標

2

A：要不要來根煙？

B：不用，謝謝。請繼續。

A：好的，我了解您時間緊迫。所以，我們就靜下心來討論，你看如何？

B：沒問題。我對你們這個月，在「汽車」雜誌廣告的新型客車，感到興趣。

A：你想你們公司會買多少輛車？

B：二、三百輛吧。

3

A：我正要找家合適的代理商，來代表我們公司。

B：你們公司生產膠底運動鞋，對不對？

A：那是我們其中一項產品—— 我們還有好幾樣運動用品。

B：我曉得。你們品牌的需求量，在本地急速成長。

A：我想你們公司正是合作的人選。

B：我很樂意加以考慮。

---

put out 生產

sneakers〔ˈsnikəz〕*n. pl.* 膠底運動鞋

4

A : We'd like to manufacture and sell your products under
your license in Taiwan.

B : Do you want to sell the products under our brand-
name?

A : Yes, we think it would be safe. Your name is quite
well-known in our country.

B : Perhaps we can help you out. Mr. Parker *spoke* very
highly of your firm.

A : Thank you. We'll *try* our *best to* introduce your
products.

SUPPLEMENTARY DIALOGS——

A : We plan to export our products to your country.
B : I heard your firm did a good deal of exporting.

A : What's the total amount of your annual sales?
B : For *the fiscal year* 1988 it was a little over 50
million dollars.

A : I'd like to *make a* trial *order* of one set.
B : OK. I'll send one by air within a week.

A : We must *keep* the deal *a secret*.
B : Don't worry. I won't tell anyone.

---

license, licence 〔ˈlaɪsn̩s〕 *n.* 許可
speak highly of 贊揚
deal 〔 dil 〕 *n.* 交易
annual 〔ˈænjʊəl 〕 *adj.* 一年的

4

A：我們想要得到貴公司許可，在台灣生產並銷售貴公司的產品。

B：你要用我們商標，去賣東西嗎？

A：對，我們想這樣會比較安全。你們的名氣在我們國家，頗爲響亮。

B：或許我們能協助你們完成。派克先生對貴公司評價很高。

A：謝謝您。我們會盡力引介你們的產品。

補充會話————————————————

A：我們計劃把我們的產品，外銷到貴國。

B：我聽說你們公司出口生意不錯。

A：你們公司年度銷售，總額有多少？

B：一九八八年會計年度，總額是五千多萬美元。

A：我想先試訂一套。

B：好的，一週內我會空運一套給你。

A：我們交易必需保守秘密。

B：別擔心，我不會告訴任何人。

---

make a trial order 試訂一套

air〔 er 〕 *v.* 空運

fiscal year 會計年度

keep sth. a secret 守密

BUSINESS ADVICE

說到 品牌，如果產品是名牌，只要一提牌子，馬上就可以得到別人對該產品品質的信賴。因此，爲了公司將來的發展，在國際市場上建立自己的品牌，是企業界首要之務。

以前 brand 是指有前科的犯人所留下的「印記」或「汚名」，現在卻轉變成具有正面意義的單字。舉例來說，「某公司的產品是台灣的 best brands」是對該公司最大的讚美，而 " brand new " 則有嶄新，令人產生好感的意思。

Do you handle the dry cell of the 'A' brand?
（你用A廠牌的乾電池嗎？）

I'm sorry we don't. But the 'B' brand is more
popular these days.
（抱歉，我們不用。不過，最近B廠牌的乾電池比較
受歡迎。）

在以上例句中，「A公司的產品」、「B公司的產品」，用英文來說，就變成了 " A brand "，" B brand "。而所謂 brand 並非僅只商品本身而已，甚至可以藉此鑑定出商品的品質。舉例來說，

What's your favorite brand ?

（你最喜歡抽那種牌子的香煙？）

"Kent" is my favorite brand.

（肯特牌是我最喜歡的香煙。）

在這段關於抽煙的對話中，我們反而不用" cigarette "（香煙）這個字眼，卻以 brand 來取代 cigarette。

◉ 技術合作

談到品牌，不得不提我們企業界一向熱衷的「技術合作」。所謂「技術合作」是指合作雙方立於對等立場，不過就我國而言，大部份情形是有一方提出較多的技術援助，而接受援助的另一方，一般而言，都要付出商標專利的租用金。如果想要製造有商標專利的商品，必須要有技術方面的情報，才能付諸製造，而第一步工作就是，要獲得專利權的契約。**授予專利權**的一方叫" *licensor* "，而**接受的一方**叫" *licensee* "，**所簽訂的契約**則稱作" *licensing a-greement* "。

To Be Continued ......

PART 2

Business Negotiation

商務交渉

LESSON 6

Describing Products

MODEL DIALOGS ─────────────

1

A : These are our new models.

B : *What are their strong points?*

A : There's a lot to be said for them. In the first place, they are more durable than any similar ones on the market.

B : Why does it take longer to wear out than the others?

A : The yarn is carefully selected for quality and woven very tightly in this fabric.

B : *Can you leave these samples with us?*

A : *How long do you want to keep them?*

B : About two weeks.

───────────────

strong point 優點
durable〔ˈdjʊrəbḷ〕*adj.* 耐用的

第六課

描述產品

對話範例 —————————————

1

A：這是我們的新樣品。

B：有什麼優點？

A：優點很多。首先，他們比市場上任何類似產品，來得耐用。

B：為什麼它比其他產品耐用呢？

A：這紗的品質是經過小心挑選，而且質地織得很緊密。

B：可以把樣品留下來嗎？

A：你要留多久？

B：大約兩星期。

---

yarn〔jɑrn〕*n.* 紗

weave〔wiv〕*v.* 編織（*pt.* wove〔wov〕*pp.* woven〔'wovən〕）

fabric〔'fæbrɪk〕*n.* 質地；布

2

A : ***What's the measurement*** ?

B : This has 1.5kg per ten pack bag.

A : How do you pack them ?

B : Ten pieces in a paper box ; 20 boxes in a wooden case.

A : What is the measurement of one case ?

B : Eight ***cubic feet*** per case.

A : I see.

3

A : This is our latest product.

B : The finish is superb. How strong is it ?

A : It's about $15\,kg/cm^2$, ***twice as strong as*** the usual one.

B : What kind of shapes do you have ?

A : As you see, three shapes are available.

B : I think it's an excellent product.

A : I'm happy to hear that.

---

measurement 〔 ˈmɛʒəmənt 〕 *n.* 度量方法

cubic 〔 ˈkjubɪk 〕 *adj.* 立方體的

cubic foot 立方呎

2

A：這大小怎麼算？

B：每十袋重一公斤半。

A：如何包裝？

B：一個紙盒裏有十件；一個木箱有二十盒。

A：一個木箱體積有多大？

B：八立方呎。

A：知道了。

3

A：這是我們最新的產品。

B：成品好極了。它的強度是多少呢？

A：大約每平方公分可以承受十五公斤的壓力，是平常產品的兩倍。

B：有那些式樣呢？

A：就你看到的，有三個式樣。

B：我認為它是項優良產品。

A：很高興聽見你這樣說。

---

superb〔su'pɝb,sə-〕*adj.* 極好的

twice as strong as sth. 比某物強一倍

4

A : How many colors are available for this item?

B : We have two standard colors. *What color do you prefer* ?

A : I prefer lighter one. Then it will *cater* more *to* teenagers.

B : I agree. If the quantity is 10,000 sets or more, you may choose any color you like.

A : *How much can you supply per month* ?

B : Our *monthly production capacity* is 50,000 sets.

SUPPLEMENTARY DIALOGS ——

A : What's the material ?

B : This is *made of* goat leather.

A : How many designs do you have ?

B : We have three designs in that grade.

A : Would it be possible to change the product slightly ?

B : Yes, it's possible. How do you want it changed?

A : That's all I have to tell you about our latest model.

B : Thank you.

---

cater〔'ketɚ〕*v.* 迎合
cater to sb. 迎合某人

4

A：這件貨品有多少種顏色？

B：有兩種標準顏色。你偏好哪一種？

A：我比較喜歡淺色的那一種。那會比較迎合十幾歲的青少年。

B：我同意。如果訂購量超過一萬件，貴公司可以選擇喜歡的顏色。

A：貴公司一個月可以供應多少貨品？

B：我們的月產量是五萬件。

補充會話

A：它的質料是什麼？

B：是山羊皮做的。

A：你們有多少種設計？

B：那一級的產品有三種設計。

A：能不能稍微修改這個產品？

B：可以呀，要怎麼修改呢？

A：關於我們最新產品，這是我得告訴你的全部內容。

B：謝謝你。

BUSINESS ADVICE

　　產品說明書，大致可分爲對產品本身的解說，及產品的使用說明兩大部分。以下用電話機爲例，把向顧客展示產品的一些要領，以圖示表現出來，希望讀者能舉一反三，將要領應用在自己銷售的產品上。

a) 產品解說（ Description ）

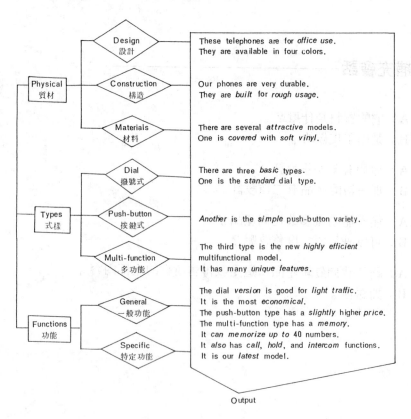

Output

b) 操作方法（ Operation ）

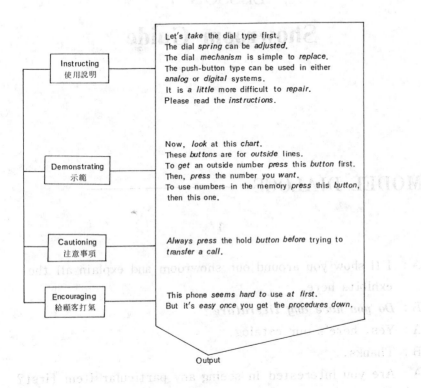

Instructing 使用説明	Let's *take* the dial type first. The dial *spring* can be *adjusted*. The dial *mechanism* is simple to *replace*. The push-button type can be used in either *analog* or *digital* systems. It is *a little* more difficult to *repair*. Please read the *instructions*.
Demonstrating 示範	Now, *look* at this *chart*. These *buttons* are for *outside* lines. To *get* an outside number *press* this *button* first. Then, *press* the number you *want*. To use numbers in the memory *press* this *button*, then this one.
Cautioning 注意事項	*Always press* the hold *button before* trying to *transfer a call*.
Encouraging 給顧客打氣	This phone *seems hard to* use at *first*. But it's *easy* once you get the *procedures down*.

Output

LESSON 7

Showroom Guide

MODEL DIALOGS ─────────────

1

A : I'll show you around our showroom and explain all the exhibits here.

B : *Do you have any literature* ?

A : Yes, here's our catalog.

B : Thanks.

A : Are you interested in seeing any particular item first?

B : No. I want to see everything.

A : Then, shall we begin viewing the objects from over there on the left ?

---

exhibit 〔 ɪgˈzɪbɪt 〕 *n.* 展覽品

literature 〔ˈlɪtərətʃɚ〕 *n.* 說明書

第七課

參觀展覽室

對話範例

1

A：讓我帶你到我們的展覽室四處看看，同時向你解說這裏所有的展覽品。

B：你有說明書嗎？

A：有，這是本公司的目錄。

B：謝謝。

A：您有興趣先看看任何特別的東西嗎？

B：不，我想看每一樣東西。

A：那麼，我們就從左邊開始參觀，好嗎？

2

A : Can I interest you in this model? This has just come out.

B : Could you demonstrate it?

A : Sure. All you have to do is *turn* it *on* and press the play button.

B : Simple enough!

A : Yes, this will really *go over* big. Would you like to try it yourself?

3

A : How many items do you have?

B : We market about 80 different items; 120 if we include the *trial products*.

A : *That's impressive*.

B : There's something I'd like to show you. This is still *at the experimental stage*.

A : What is the power source of this robot?

B : It has *dry cell batteries*. Let me show you some of its features.

---

demonstrate〔'dɛmən,stret〕*vt*. 示範

turn on 打開開關

go over 成功

trial product 試驗性產品

2

A：讓我向你介紹這個樣品，才剛推出的。

B：能示範如何使用嗎？

A：當然可以。你只要打開開關，然後按啓動鍵就可以了。

B：眞夠簡單！

A：對呀，這產品眞的會大大地成功。想不想自己來試一試？

3

A：貴公司有多少種產品？

B：我們在市場上銷售的有八十種，如果包括試驗性產品，就有一百二十種。

A：眞令人佩服！

B：有件東西想給你瞧瞧。這還在實驗階段。

A：這機器人的電源在哪裏呢？

B：它配備有乾電池。讓我告訴你它的特點。

---

at the experimental stage 在試驗階段

robot〔'robət,'rɑb-〕*n.* 機器人

dry cell battery 乾電池

4

A : Did you enjoy visiting our showroom?

B : Yes, I did. You have a lot of attractive merchandise.

A : Thank you. I hope you'll place some orders before you leave.

B : I'll *run through* your catalog and make a list of what we*'re likely to* want.

A : I see. Thank you for sparing your precious time.

B : Thank you for all the information.

SUPPLEMENTARY DIALOGS ——

A : Thank you for coming to our exhibition today.

B : I'm happy to be here. I intend to take a good look at your products.

A : Please feel free to ask me anything.

B : Yes, I will.

A : *How long is the warranty good for* ?

B : Two years, Mr.X. Within that period, all repairs are free.

A : Now this is the last item for today.

B : That's very interesting.

---

merchandise〔ˈmɝtʃən‚daɪz〕 *n.* 商品
run through 很快地看過

4

A：參觀我們的展覽室，還滿意吧？

B：是的。你們很多貨品都相當吸引人。

A：謝謝。希望您在離開前會留下些訂單。

B：我會很快看過目錄，列表寫下可能要買的貨品。

A：知道了。佔用您寶貴的時間——謝謝您。

B：也謝謝您提供的資訊。

補充會話 ─────────────────────

A：謝謝您今天蒞臨我們的展覽會。

B：很高興來到這裏。我想好好參觀你們的產品。

A：請隨意發問。

B：我會的。

A：保證期限多久？

B：X先生，兩年。在這段期間內，所有修理都是免費的。

A：好了，這是今天最後一項貨品。

B：真有趣。

---

be likely to 可能　　***good for***（*two year*）保證期限為（二年）

warranty〔ˈwɔrəntɪ, ˈwɑr-〕*n.* 保證期限

BUSINESS ADVICE

當你 帶領顧客到展覽室，你可以說：

Please come this way. I'd like to show you our show-room.

（請走這邊。我想帶你參觀我們的展覽室。）

I'll take you to our showroom.

（我會帶你到我們的展示室。）

Let me show you around our showroom.

（讓我帶你到我們展覽室四處看看。）

最後一句 " around " 之後的單字可自行轉換應用。譬如：當我們要帶客人參觀自己家的時候，可以說：

Let me show you around my house.

（讓我向你介紹這項產品。）

如果 有意說動顧客，買下某件特定產品時，可用：

Can I interest you in this one？

（讓我向你介紹這項產品。）

簡單的說：則可以用：

How about this one？

What about this one？

（這東西如何？）

爲了 減少顧客對品質的懷疑，適時美言幾句，增加顧客對品質的信賴，是絕對有必要的。推銷襯衫時，我們可以說：

We have some fine shirts here. We **guarantee** its quality.
（我們這裏有幾件上好的襯衫，品質保證。）

這句裏用了"guarantee"這個字，它比中文的「保證」，語感來得強烈多了。當我們對使用期限，提出保證時，便可以說：

We'll quarantee this product for one year.
（我們這項產品保用一年。）

　　　　　*　　　　　*　　　　　*

當然，也可以代換成"warrant"這個字。如：

We'll warrant this product for three years.

想要表示"推薦產品"或者"保證商品品質"，這類語意的時候，則可用"endorse"這個字。如：

We can endorse this model.
（我們推薦這型的產品。）

最後，當顧客要離開的時候，千萬別忘了說：

Thank you for giving us your precious time.
（謝謝您給我們寶貴的時間。）

I'm very glad to have met you. I hope to see you again.
（非常高興認識你。希望跟你再見面。）

LESSON 8
Price Negotiation

MODEL DIALOGS —————————

1

A : Is this your best price ?

B : I'm afraid it is. That's our *rock-bottom price*.

A : That may be true, but if you make it cheaper, we'll be able to place large orders continuously.

B : About what price would you say ?

A : I have to ask you for $9.00.

B : $9.00 is *out of the question*. The best I can offer you is $9.50.

——————————————

best price 最優惠的價格
rock-bottom price 底價

第八課

討價還價

對話範例

1

A：這是最優惠的價格嗎？

B：恐怕就這樣了。那是我們的底價。

A：也許眞的如此，但如果你能算便宜點，我們後續會有大批定單。

B：你開個價吧！

A：九塊錢。

B：九塊錢，不可能啦。最便宜算你九塊半。

---

out of the question 不可能的

2

A : The prices you quoted us are a little too high. I want
   a 20% discount.
B : I can't give a reduction like that !
A : Look, I know you can manage that. I've already had a
   similar offer from your competitors.
B : But when it comes to quality, there's no comparison.
A : You have to meet my figure, if your company really
   wants to sell more.
B : Well, I need some time to think it over.

3

A : We've had to increase our prices on some of our
   items.
B : Up again ?
A : Yes. However, since the quality has also improved,
   the raise is justifiable.
B : How much has it *gone up* ?
A : The unit price has been raised by 5% to $27.
B : I didn't expect it to go that high.

---

quote〔kwot〕*vt.* 報價
20% discount 八折

2

A：你定的價格有點太高。我要這個價碼的八折。

B：我不能給這種折扣！

A：嘿，我知道你能處理。你的競爭對手已經給我類似的價格。

B：可是如果講到品質，這就沒得比了。

A：如果你的公司真想多賣一些，就得遷就我的價格。

B：唔，我需要點時間考慮。

3

A：我們某些產品價格得略作調整。

B：又要漲價了嗎？

A：是的。既然品質已有改進，漲價也是理所當然。

B：要漲多少呢？

A：單價上漲百分之五，二十七塊。

B：我沒想到會漲得那麼高。

---

justifiable〔ˈdʒʌstəˌfaɪəbḷ〕*adj.* 理所當然的
go up 增加

4

A : How much are you asking per unit?

B : Our factory price is $4.50 per unit. But it depends on quantity.

A : Assume I order 30,000 outright?

B : Then I could bring it down to $4.48.

A : That doesn't seem like much of a reduction. How about $4.45?

B : I'll tell you what. *If you double the order, I suppose we could consider it.*

SUPPLEMENTARY DIALOGS———

A : How much can you bring the price down?

B : *I'm afraid that there is no room to negotiate the price.*

A : They look rather steep.

B : Yes, but they are worth that much.

A : How much are the prices up?

B : About 5 percent on the average.

A : If you won't come down to $23, we won't buy one.

B : I'm sorry, but *I cannot make any further discounts.*

---

factory price 工廠定價
assume〔ə'sjum〕*v.* 假定
outright〔'aʊt'raɪt〕*adv.* 總共地

4

A：請問單價多少？

B：我們工廠單價是四塊半。但可依訂購量稍作調整。

A：假設我總共要訂三萬件呢？

B：那麼可以降價到四點四八元。

A：折扣不怎麼多嘛。四點四五元如何？

B：這麼說好了，如果你訂單加倍，我想，我們倒可以考慮。

補充會話─────────────────

A：你還能便宜多少？

B：恐怕已經沒辦法再討價還價了。

A：這些價錢看起來很不合理。

B：是呀，但是他們就是值這麼多錢。

A：漲多少錢？

B：平均漲百分之五。

A：如果價格不低於二十三塊，我們就不會買。

B：抱歉，實在不能再打折了。

---

steep〔stip〕*adj*.（價格）過份；不合理

average〔'ævərɪdʒ〕*n*. 平均

discount〔'dɪskaʊnt〕*n*. 折扣

BUSINESS ADVICE

表 達價格高低，可像形容「山」一樣，使用 " *high* " 和 " *low* " 二個字。譬如：

That's too high.

（價錢太高了。）

Oh, no, this is the lowest price.

（噢，不，這是最低價。）

也可以用比喻性說法。如：

Let us have your rock-bottom price.

（給我們您的底價。）

所謂的 " *rock-bottom price* "，是誇張地表示，價格已經十分低，已經跌到了谷底。

談到價錢，我們還常用 " *reasonable* " 這個形容詞，簡單地說，這個字的意思就是「合理」的意思。如：

The price is quite reasonable.

（這價格相當合理。）

那麼，" *unreasonable* " 則指價格很高，高得不合理。如：

The price is unreasonable.

（這價格高得不合理。）

說到價格便宜，請儘量不要用 " *cheap* " 這個字，因為它意味著商品是由廉價勞工（cheap labor）製造出來的廉價品。

你會討價還價嗎？

萬一對方價格過高，為了殺價，可以說：

Can you make it a little cheaper ?

Can you come down a little ?

Can you reduce the price ?

（你能不能算便宜一點？）

當要強調出商品品質時，使交易達到理想的價格時，我們可以
說：

This one is very good for 10 dollars.

（這東西絕對值十塊錢。）

These are slightly higher in price, but their superior
quality makes them more valuable than the less expensive ones.

（這些貨價稍微高了一點，但他們優異的品質，使它們
　比那些較便宜的貨，更有價值。）

此外，我們還可以用「 …. (all right)，but…. 」的句型來造
句，如：

The price is high but it's an unusual well made tie.
Please look at the label. It's designed by Pierre
Cardin.

（這價格是貴，不過，這是條製作精良，不尋常的領帶。
　請看看商標，是由皮爾卡登設計的。）

LESSON 9

Factory Tour Ⅰ

MODEL DIALOGS

1

A : I'll be accompanying you on your tour today.

B : Thank you for all the trouble you're going to take for me.

A : No trouble at all. I only hope I'll be able to help you.

B : I'm sure you will.

A : Here's a schedule we've prepared. I hope it's suitable for you.

B : All right. I'll be ready in five minutes.

---

accompany〔ə'kʌmpənɪ〕*vt.* 陪伴

第九課

參觀工廠㈠

對話範例

1

A：今天我會陪你參觀。
B：謝謝你替我省去一切麻煩。
A：一點也不麻煩。我只希望能幫你忙。
B：相信你會的。
A：這是我們準備好的行程表，希望合你意。
B：一切沒問題。五分鐘內，我會準備就緒。

2

A : I'll give you a little information about your itinerary for today.

B : I'd appreciate that.

A : We'll reach the plant by 10:30 and we'll be on a tour before lunch. We're scheduled to be back here in Taipei by 2:30.

B : *Could you be a little more specific?*

A : Of course. I'll be giving you more details on the way there. Now shall we start?

3

A : Mr. Brown, I'd like you to meet Mr. Lee, the plant manager.

B : How do you do, Mr. Lee?

C : How do you do, Mr. Brown? It's a pleasure to meet you.

B : The pleasure's mine.

C : I'll give you a complete picture of our operation.

B : Thank you. That's why I came.

C : First, I'll show you an 8-minute multivision.

---

itinerary〔 aɪˈtɪnə,rɛrɪ 〕 *n.* 行程；路線圖

2

A：我會針對今天行程，向你作份簡報。

B：非常感謝。

A：我們十點半以前到達工廠，午餐前會先去視察。預定下午兩點半以前返回台北。

B：能不能講更詳細些？

A：當然可以。我會在路上告訴你細節。現在可以出發了嗎？

3

A：布朗先生，容我向你引介工廠經理，李先生。

B：你好，李先生。

C：你好，布朗先生。很高興認識你。

B：這是我的榮幸。

C：我會把我們製作過程的總圖給你。

B：謝謝您。這正是我今天來的目的。

C：首先，我為您放映八分鐘的多媒體簡介。

---

multivision〔ˌmʌltɪˈvɪʒən〕*n.* 多媒體

4

A : When was this factory founded?

B : In 1976 with a capital of 2 million dollars.

A : How many employees do you have?

B : There are about 1,200 in the plant, and 80 in the office.

A : You are expanding your plant.

B : Yes. Our new plant will start production next month.

A : That will help to *speed* things *up*.

B : Of course. It has taken two years altogether.

SUPPLEMENTARY DIALOGS——

A : I hope the noise isn't bothering you.

B : No, not at all. *I'm accustomed to* this sort of thing.

A : If there's some place you'd like to stop, don't hesitate to ask.

B : Thank you. I'll keep that in mind.

A : I hear your plant is *phasing in* robots.

B : Yes, we began last spring.

A : These machines seem to be the most modern ones of their kind.

B : That's true. We believe that superior equipment *makes for* superior products.

---

capital〔'kæpətḷ〕*n.* 資本額
employee〔ɪm'plɔɪ‧i,ˌɛmplɔɪ'i〕*n.* 雇工
speed sth. up 增加某物的速度
be accustomed to 習慣

4

A：這家工廠何時成立？

B：一九七六年，當時資本額美元兩百萬元。

A：工廠有多少雇工？

B：工廠裏有一千兩百位工人，辦公室有八十名職員。

A：貴公司正在擴廠。

B：是的。我們的新工廠下個月開始動工生產。

A：那會有助於出貨速度加快。

B：當然了。那總共花了兩年的時間。

補充會話 ────────────────

A：希望這些噪音沒有吵到你。

B：一點也不會。我已經習慣這種聲音。

A：如果想在哪兒停下來，不要不好意思說。

B：謝謝。我會記在心裏。

A：聽說你們工廠逐漸採用機器人。

B：對，從去年春季開始的。

A：這些機器似乎是同類中最新型的。

B：沒錯。我們相信優良設備有助於生產優良產品。

---

phase in 逐漸採用

equipment〔ɪˈkwɪpmənt〕*n.* 設備

make for 有助於

BUSINESS ADVICE

帶領客戶參觀工廠時，您會使用到的一些用語：

1. I'll give you a little information on our schedule.
（關於我們的行程，我會向你做番簡報。）

I'll give you more information on the way to the factory.
（去工廠的路上，我會告訴你更多事情。）

2. We'll drive to the factory, which is about 45 minutes from here.
（我們會開車去工廠,距離大約是四十五分鐘的車程。）

3. Mr. Song will be meeting us there. He will be the one who actually shows you around.
（宋先生會在那裏等我們。他是真正要帶你到四處參觀的人。）

4. Let me take you around the factory.
（讓我帶你到工廠四處看看。）

The power plant was built 5 years ago.
（這座電力廠是五年前建立的。）

At present, there are 967 workers at the manufacturing plant.
（目前，這座製造廠有員工九百六十七人。）

5. Watch your step.
（當心您的腳步！）

I'm not familiar with that point. Let me call someone who is more knowledgeable.
（關於那一點我不太熟悉。讓我打電話給比較曉得情況的人。）

6. Well, shall we have a break？ You must be tired, having seen all of our plants all at once.
（好了，我們是不是應該休息一下呢？一下子參觀完我們全部的工廠，你一定累了。）

I hope you don't mind having Chinese food for lunch.
（希望你不介意午飯吃中國菜。）

7. We still have plenty of time, so if there's some place you'd like to stop by, please don't hesitate to ask.
（我們還有很多時間，所以如果你想到哪裏逗留，請不要不好意思說。）

8. We're running a little short on time, so....
（我們時間有點不夠，所以…。）

I hope you found the trip informative.
（希望你發現這趟旅行很有收穫。）

9. This completes our schedule for today.
（這完成了我們今天的行程。）

LESSON 10
Factory Tour Ⅱ

MODEL DIALOGS————————

1

A : Why don't we start at our main plant?

B : Sure. *What's your annual output*?

A : It would be approximately 800,000 tons. Production is double what it was 3 years ago.

B : *What's your market share*?

A : It was over 48% last year. We're the largest manufacturer in Taiwan in this line of business.

B : Is that right?

A : We*'re supposed to* take off shoes from here. And please use these slippers.

---

annual output 年產量

approximately〔 ə'prɑksəmɪtlɪ 〕*adv.* 大約

第十課
參觀工廠㈡

對話範例 ——————————————

1

A：何不從我們總廠開始參觀呢？

B：當然好啊。你們年產量是多少？

A：大約八十萬噸，是三年前的兩倍。

B：市場佔有率如何？

A：去年超過百分之四十八。我們是台灣同業中，最大的製造商。

B：是嗎？

A：我們應該在這裏脫鞋。這裏有脫鞋，請穿。

——————————————

be supposed to 應該

2

A: What is your usual percentage of rejects?

B: In normal operations it would be about 6 or 7 percent. But in our factory it's only 3.9 percent.

A: That's fantastic.

B: Our quality control is very strict.

A: How much do you spend on R & D?

B: About 3 percent of gross sales. Please come along and see our R & D Department.

3

A: Everybody is working very hard.

B: Yes. We are short-handed.

A: I've heard Taiwan is one of the countries with the densest population.

B: Nevertheless, we are short of laborers these days.

A: They take home excellent salaries, I hope.

B: That's right. Taiwan is no longer a nation of cheap labor.

---

percentage of rejects 退貨率

R & D（Research and Development） 研究發展

gross sale 銷售總量

2

A：你們通常退貨率是多少？

B：一般工廠正常操作，退貨率是百分之六到百分之七。而我們工廠只有百分之三點九。

A：很棒嘛。

B：我們品管非常嚴格。

A：你們花費多少錢在研究發展上？

B：大約是銷售總量的百分之三。請隨我來，參觀我們的研發部。

3

A：每個人都非常努力工作。

B：是啊，人手不夠。

A：聽說台灣是人口最稠密的國家之一。

B：然而，我們最近人手還是不夠。

A：希望他們拿回家的是高薪。

B：沒錯，台灣已經不再是個廉價勞工的國家。

---

short-handed 人手不足的

dense〔dɛns〕*adj.* 稠密的

4

A : What do you think of our factory?

B : I'm very favorably impressed. I think we may be able to work together.

A : I'm very glad to hear that. We'll work very hard to **live up to** your expectations.

B : I'll do my best, too.

A : Well, shall we **have a break**?

B : Good idea.

SUPPLEMENTARY DIALOGS —

A : Can you give me more details on that?

B : I'd be happy to.

A : Did you get the information you were after?

B : Actually, I got far more than I had expected.

A : Thank you very much for the tour.

B : Not at all. I'm sorry I couldn't answer all of your questions better.

A : Can you explain it more in detail?

B : I'm sorry, but the technical know-how is confidential.

---

live up to 達到預期標準

4

A：您對我們工廠印象如何？

B：印象深刻，非常佩服。我想，我們或許能一塊兒合作。

A：很高興聽到這個消息。我們將會非常努力工作，以達成你的期望。

B：我也會盡力。

A：好了，讓我們稍作休息吧！

B：好主意。

補充會話 ——————————————

A：能不能說得更詳細些？

B：樂意之至。

A：你得到要追查的消息嗎？

B：實際上，我得到的比預期的，多得多。

A：非常感謝安排這次參觀。

B：別客氣。抱歉不能更詳細回答你所有的問題。

A：你能再解釋詳細一點嗎？

B：抱歉，技術上的秘訣，事屬機密（恕不奉告）。

---

have a break 稍作休息

techinical know-how 技術上的秘訣

confidential〔͵kɑnfəˈdɛnʃəl〕*adj*. 機密的

BUSINESS ADVICE

説服 歐美客戶，其中很重要的一種方法就是，提供詳細的統計資料。使用「稍微」、「大概這個程度左右」，這一類的話，是無法取得對方的信賴。正確地列出公司的**銷售量、生產量、市場佔有率、退貨率**，以及**研究開發費用**等，是絕對有必要的。以年度銷售額爲例：

What's the total amount of your annual sales?
（請問您公司年度總銷售額是多少？）

For the fiscal year 1988 it was a little over 300 million dollars.
（一九八八年會計年度，銷售額小幅突破三億元。）

單純 僅計算賣出的金額是不夠的，**利潤**的計算也很重要。如果想問「利潤多少？」的時候，您可以這麼問：

What's the percentage of your profit?
（您的利潤有幾成？）

What's the total profit of your annual sales?
（您整年銷售，總收益是多少？）

銷售，可依地區範圍不同，分爲兩類：經營國內銷售，叫做“*domestic sales*”，如果是經營出口業務的話，

則稱爲 " *overseas sales* " 或是 " *sales abroad* "。瞭解這兩個術語之後，自然對以下例句的意義，就能輕易掌握了。例句：

What's the percentage of overseas markets in proportion to domestic markets for your product ?
（你產品的內銷與外銷比例是多少呢？）

The ratio is about 7 overseas to 3 domestic.
（七成外銷，三成內銷。）

詢問 生產量時，可以這麼說：

What's your annual output ?
（您年產量是多少？）

Here's a pamphlet about this plant's yearly production.
（這本小冊子是有關這家工廠的年度產品介紹。）

如果問「占有市場多少個百分比」，則是問該產品的
市場佔有率，即所謂的 *market share* 。例如：

What's your market share ?
（你們的市場佔有率是多少？）

What's the market share held by your company ?
（你們公司控制的市場佔有率是多少？）

To Be Continued ......

PART 3

Nearing an Agreement
契約將成

LESSON 11

Terms of Payment

MODEL DIALOGS —————————

1

A : Now I'd like to go over the *terms of payment*.

B : What do you have in mind?

A : Full payment must be made at the time of the shipment.

B : Hmm.

A : We've already reduced the price by 3%. Please keep that in mind.

B : All right. I see no problem.

A : I appreciate your cooperation.

---

terms of payment 付款條件

第十一課

付款條件

對話範例

1

A：現在我想討論付費條件。
B：你心裏有什麼腹案呢？
A：所有款項得在裝船時付清。
B：嗯。
A：我們已經降價百分之三。請記得這一點。
B：好吧，我看沒問題。
A：感謝您的合作。

---

cooperation〔koˌɑpəˈreʃən〕*n.* 合作

2

A : I wonder if you could consider spreading payment over a period of time.

B : Do you mean installment payments?

A : Right.

B : If you insist, we may be able to consider that type of payment.

A : How does it work?

B : Generally, 10% down and the balance is to be divided in three equal monthly payments.

3

A : (*On the phone*) What do you think of our proposition regarding payment?

B : Basically, I think it's reasonable. But the first payment is more than we expected.

A : Please consider our ***profit margin***. It isn't large.

B : But I'd appreciate a more favorable condition.

A : Well, I'll have to give it some more thought.

B : When can I have an answer?

A : I'll let you know within an hour.

---

installment〔ɪn'stɔlmənt〕*n.* 分期付款

balance〔'bæləns〕*n.* 餘款

2

A：我想，或許你可以接受，把錢分攤在一段時間付。

B：你是說分期付款嗎？

A：對。

B：如果你堅持的話，我們也許可以考慮這樣的付款方式。

A：怎麼算呢？

B：一般都是先付一成，餘款分三個月付清。

3

A：（電話中）您對我們建議的付款方法有什麼意見？

B：基本上，我想蠻合理的。但是頭期款比我們想像得還多。

A：請考慮我們的利潤，並不多。

B：但是，如果能有更優惠的條件，我會很感激。

A：好吧，我一定會多考慮考慮。

B：什麼時候給我答覆？

A：一個小時以內。

---

profit margin 利潤

4

A : We're in a tough position. Please consider *D/P payment* .

B : As I said before, I'd like to. But I can't get permission from the company.

A : Can't you think it over a little more?

B : I'm afraid we just can't.

A : Come on.... Isn't there anything that could be done?

B : Sorry, it's out of my hands now.

SUPPLEMENTARY DIALOGS———

A : What are your terms of payment?

B : Please open *an irrevocable confirmed L/C* at sight.

A : Please give us a quotation in US dollars for model No.5.

B : It is around US $40 *C.I.F.* London. The payment term is *cash on delivery* .

A : What about the cost of delivery?

B : We'd like to do it in accordance with an *F.O.B.*

A : Can you tell me the advising bank of your *L/C* and its number?

B : The *advising bank* is the First Bank head office which is to confirm the L/C, and its number is 523.

D/P payment (Deferred Payment) 延期付款

C.I.F. (Cost, Insurance and Freight) 包括保險運費的價格

cash on delivery 交貨收款

4

A：我們公司有困難。請考慮讓我們延期付款。

B：我以前說過，我很想。但是公司不批准。

A：難道不能多考慮一下？

B：恐怕就是不能。

A：別這樣嘛。難道一點忙也不能幫嗎？

B：抱歉，現在不歸我管。

補充會話 ——————————————

A：你們的付款條件是什麼？

B：請立刻開立一張不可取銷信用狀。

A：請給我五號模型美元的價格表。

B：到倫敦，包括保險運費的價格，大約是美金四十元。貨到請即付現。

A：運費大約多少？

B：隨船上交貨價調整。

A：能告訴您信用狀的通知銀行，以及信用狀號碼嗎？

B：通知銀行是第一銀行總行，它認可過。信用狀號碼是 523。

F.O.B.（free on board）船上交貨價

advising bank 通知銀行

L／C（letter of credit）信用狀

BUSINESS ADVICE

在 日常會話中，詢問價格使用How much is this？就足夠了。但是在商談貿易事務的對話中，就沒有這麼簡單了。由於商品運送的路途十分遙遠，像運費、保險費由哪一邊負擔？以及在哪裏收受貨物？等等條件都必須事先訂定言明，才能知道價格到底是高還是低。試看以下這組對話：

A : And the price？
（價格是多少呢？）

B : Twenty cents per yard.
（一碼要二十分錢。）

A : On what term？
（運費怎麼算呢？）

B : F.O.B. Keelung.
（在基隆交貨，運費、保險費由賣方負擔。）

A : That's too high. I thought it was on a C.I.F basis.
（太貴了。我以為運費、保險費都已經算在貨款裏了。）

◎ 入境問俗學術語

在 運送貨品中，*F.O.B.* 是指貨品由輸出港運出的方式，是*free on board*（賣方免費運送）。因此，所謂 "*F.O.B. Kee-*

lung "就是指在基隆交貨，其間運貨、保險費**由賣方付**。相反地，**C.I.F.** 是 *cost, insurance and freight* 的縮寫,意思是由輸出港口一直到目的地為止，其間的運費及保險費都包括在貨款之內。使用 **C.I.F.** 時，也必須要指定地名，如 "**C.I.F. Seatle**",是指由西雅圖輸出，到目的地為止，其間的運費、保險費都包含在貨款之中，**由買主來付**。一般而言，如用 **F.O.B.** 對進口商比較保險,**C.I.F.** 則對出口商比較保險。

⬤ MONEY *!* MONEY *!* MONEY *!*

支 付貨款，如同國內交易有**現金、支票、賒帳**等不同方式，在進出口貿易上,除了一般以滙票進行交易之外,也有所謂「預先付款」(*payment in advance*)或是「貨到付款」(*cash on delivery*)不同方式。使用滙票(*documentary draft*)交易時，購買者必須透過銀行開立信用狀(*L/C = letter of credit*)，交給賣方，賣方再依信用狀，於裝貨後開立滙票，所以很少有收不到貨的情形發生。附帶一提的是，滙票具有**見票即付**(*pay at sight*)及**延後付款**時間(*usance*)的特性，可用 60 *d/s* 的方式表示,意思是見票後六十天付款。(*d/s = day after sight*)。

☆☆Quiz：請寫出下列術語的意思：

F.O.B（ free on board ）

C.I.F.（ cost, insurance and freight ）

documentary draft

L/C（ letter of credit ）

usance   90 d/s

pay at sight   pay in advance

LESSON 12

Terms of Delivery

MODEL DIALOGS————————————

1

A : What quantities would you order?

B : Can you make around 80,000 pieces in this mold?

A : We've got only 50,000 pieces at the present time. When do you need them?

B : Please rush this order.

A : I'll arrange to have them reach you in five days. Would that be satisfactory?

B : Good. You must deliver the goods in that time.

A : Don't worry about it. We can come up with your order.

---

come up with 趕得上

第十二課
送貨用語

對話範例 ────────────────

1

A：你想訂多少貨？

B：這一型，大約八萬件，你能供應嗎？

A：現在我們手邊只有五萬件。你什麼時候要？

B：盡快。

A：我們安排讓貨五天內到你那兒去。您滿意嗎？

B：好。你必須在那時把貨送到。

A：別擔心，趕得上您的訂單。

2

A : What quantity do you have in mind?

B : Thirty thousand dozen in five shipments.

A : When do you want to start and how do you want it shipped?

B : Six thousand dozen each month for five months starting in July will be fine.

A : In October, the production line is very busy. So, if we could ship 3,000 dozen in October, then we'll **make** it **up** by sending 9,000 dozens in November.

B : Okay, but you've gotta be sure to meet it.

3

A : (*On the phone*) Could we get them delivered by the end of this month?

B : It's rather difficult... we have now a rush of orders and we are working **round the clock.**

A : **What is the present lead time**, then?

B : I'm afraid it'll be about four to six months. If you need immediate shipment, you'll have to check stocks of other manufacturers.

A : I see. We'll find another supplier.

B : Please understand that immediate shipment after an order is not possible.

2

A：你心裏想訂多少貨？

B：三萬打，分五船裝運。

A：你要什麼時候開船？如何裝運？

B：每月六千打，分五個月送，從七月開始即可。

A：十月生產線會很忙。所以，可能的話，我們十月送三千打，到十一月再補送九千打。

B：可以，但你得確定要趕得及。

3

A：（電話中）月底可以送到嗎？

B：有點困難…我們有些訂單要趕，正在日夜加班。

A：那麼，目前最快要什麼時候？

B：恐怕要四到六個月以後。如果你馬上需要船運，你得要查查其他製造商的存貨。

A：我知道，我會找別家供應商。

B：請多諒解，一份訂單要馬上裝運是不可能辦得到的。

---

make up 彌補過來
round the clock 日夜加班
supplier〔səˈplaɪə〕*n.* 供應商

4

A : (*On the phone*) How long will it take to get the sample?

B : It'll take about 30 days to send it *by ship*.

A : It's too late.

B : Then I'll have it *rushed off* to you *by air*.

A : That would be better.

B : How soon can you give me the order details?

A : When I receive the sample, I'll send you the *purchase order*.

SUPPLEMENTARY DIALOGS———

A : When can you deliver the goods?

B : Within 3 months upon arrival of your L/C.

A : Do you have SM-3s in stock?

B : Yes. We always try to *keep on* adequate stock.

A : Can you *fill this order*?

B : Yes, we have enough stocks to supply you.

A : I'm afraid I'll have to reconsider the order.

B : Why do you say so?

---

rush off 趕

purchase order 定購單

keep on 保持

4

A：（電話中）要多久才能拿到樣本？
B：船運要三十天。
A：太晚了。
B：那麼用空運趕送給你。
A：那比較理想。
B：要多久才能給我訂單細目呢？
A：我收到樣本後，就會把定購單寄給你。

補充會話 ————————————

A：何時送貨運來？
B：你信用狀送達後三個月以內。

A：你有 SM-3S 的存貨嗎？
B：有。我們一直試圖保持存貨充裕。

A：你能接下這份訂單嗎？
B：可以，我們有足夠的存貨供應。

A：恐怕我得再重新考慮這份訂單。
B：爲什麼這麼說呢？

---

stock〔stɑk〕*n.* 存貨
fill the order 接下定單

BUSINESS ADVICE

◉ 填填看 1 GROSS = ___DOZENS = ___PIECES

　　貨品數量單位上，可分作 *piece*（件，個），*dozen*（打），*gross*（籮）等。一般而言，*dozen* 是指**十二個**，*gross* 是指**一百四十四個**即十二打。但由於商品種類不同，會有些許的差異，必須加以留意。舉例來說，" *baker's dozen* "，在糕餅業是指**十三個**，因為古代對重量不足的規定十分嚴格，因此當時業者，乾脆一打多加一個，以符合規定，流傳至今，" *baker's dozen* "變成了特殊的習慣用法，指的是十三個，而不是一般的一打十二個。

** dozen 是單位名稱，因而有下列重要句型產生：

Sell by the dozen.
（論打賣，一打一打地賣。）

Cheaper by the dozen.
（整打買，算便宜點。）

◉ 五噸煤炭的故事

重量單位，英美制也略有不同。英國的噸（*English ton*）是長噸（*long ton*），有 2240 磅，比公制的噸（*metric ton*）2204 磅來得重。而美制的噸叫做短噸（*short ton*），只有兩千磅，比 metric ton 來得輕。

英國人、美國人之間，就曾爲了計算五噸煤炭的多少，引起過不小的紛爭。英國方面由於煤炭用完了，而向美國方面採購，以求補充原料。但是英國買主所要的五噸煤炭是指英噸，而賣方美國人卻用「美噸」來估量，以致於產生了近一成的差額，這可說是由於英美雙方習慣不同，造成誤解的例子。因此，爲避免誤會產生，應事先採取方法防範這類爭端。

雙方應採用彼此都認同的單位,不管是用箱(*case*)、包(*bale*)、袋(*bag*)或綑(*bundle*)爲單位，買賣雙方對於每單位中的個數，或是內容物的總重量等，都必須取得共識。總重量（*gross weight*）減去包裝的重量（*tare*）就是淨重（*net*），原理雖然非常簡單，但是在貿易上，由於貨物要長途搬運，起運時的重量（*shipped weight*）和到達時的重量（*landed weight*），其間難免有差距。唯有雙方先取得協議，才能避免誤解。舉例來說，要避免貨物重量短少，所產生的糾紛,就可事先訂立契約,明文規定:

Loss in weight over 2% will be for seller's account.
（重量損失超過百分之二總重的部分，歸賣方負擔。）

在契約中可預估重量可能的增減，明定雙方的責任範圍，而插入像「重量增減以不超出總重的百分之十爲限」，這一類的話，也就是所謂的 "*more or less term*"。

LESSON 13

Establishing an Agreement

MODEL DIALOGS ───────────

1

A : (*On the phone*) Have you come to any decision ?

B : No, not yet. We're still talking it over.

A : When will you give us a definite answer ?

B : Well, let's not be hasty. We're having a board meeting to *nail* it *down*.

A : I hope we shall be able to work together.

B : I hope so, too. I'll contact you after the meeting is over.

---

establish 〔 ə'stæblɪʃ 〕 *vt.* 訂立

agreement 〔 ə'grimənt 〕 *n.* 契約

第十三課

訂立契約

對話範例

1

A：（電話中）你們作成了任何決議嗎？

B：還沒有。我們還在討論。

A：什麼時候可以給我們明確答覆？

B：嘿，別趕嘛。我們要開董事會議，才能定案。

A：希望我們可以一起工作。

B：我也希望如此。會議結束後，我會跟你連絡。

---

board meeting 董事會議
nail down 使成定案

2

A : You've read the summary of our negotiations. Do you see any problem?

B : No. There are no problems as far as I can see.

A : Then, it's set. Let's put it into writing and sign it.

B : Before signing, if you like, I'd like to have our consultant look at it.

A : Fine.

3

A : What do you think of this contract?

B : It's okay, up to a point.

A : What do you mean?

B : Well, I'm in agreement in principle, but there're still a few details that have to be ironed out.

A : Which points do we still differ on?

B : First of all, clause number 6. Your conditions are too severe.

A : I think that's what we agreed on.

---

consultant〔kən'sʌltənt〕 *n.* 顧問
up to a point 相當中肯

2

A：讀過我們談判的摘要，你看有沒有問題呢？

B：沒有。就目前所見，我看沒問題。

A：那麼，就這樣決定了。讓我們把它寫成書面文件，然後簽署。

B：如果你願意的話，簽字以前，我想讓我們顧問看看。

A：好的。

3

A：對這份合同有何意見？

B：不錯，蠻中肯的。

A：您的意思是——

B：嗯，大體上我同意，不過有些細節上，我們仍有歧見要消除。

A：我們在哪些地方還有歧見？

B：首先，條款第六條，您的條件太苛了。

A：我想，那是我們同意的條件。

---

iron out 消除歧見

4

A : I'm happy that we could arrive at a mutually satisfactory agreement.

B : I feel the same way. It sure took a long time.

A : I can't believe the number of times we met.

B : I didn't intend to draw out the negotiations.

A : I understand your position quite well.

B : When will the contract papers be ready?

A : I'll have them ready for you tomorrow morning.

SUPPLEMENTARY DIALOGS ——

A : Let's review what's been decided so far.

B : Good idea.

A : How long should we make the contract for?

B : Ordinarily, we make a 2-year contract.

A : Before we sign this contract, may I confirm a couple
of things?

B : Of course. What are they?

A : I guess we're all in agreement now.

B : All we have to do now is shake hands.

---

draw out 使變長

4

A：很高興我們能夠簽署，彼此都滿意的合約。

B：我也有同感。當然花了很多時間。

A：我不敢相信，我們已經見過那麼多次面。

B：我不是有意把談判拖長。

A：我非常了解你的立場。

B：合約書什麼時候準備好？

A：明天早上我會替你預備好合約書。

補充會話——————————

A：讓我們把目前已經決定的項目，再檢查一次。

B：好主意。

A：我們契約應該要簽多久？

B：通常我們是簽兩年的約。

A：在我們簽約之前，我想確定一些事，可以嗎？

B：當然可以，什麼事？

A：我想，我們現在完全達成協議。

B：現在要做的事情，就是握握手了。

BUSINESS ADVICE

像 美國由於多種民族共存，導致思考方式及價值觀的多樣化，為避免不斷的紛爭和是非，一般習慣採用**契約**（*verbal contract*），以書面形式明定出彼此的權利義務。契約的功能除了避免某些問題產生，也使個人權利範圍更加明確，

美 商對於商談中的對話一定要徹底確認，而且對於商談中雙方同意的事項，一定立刻打字記下來，當場就簽字。若是在電話中商談，則會馬上將同意事項打字，寄給對方。另外常見的還有，用來記錄商談內容的議事紀錄。若彼此能做到這種程度的確認，就是再小的紛爭也不會產生，這是我們必須學習的商業習慣。

ATTENTION!

和外國企業往來，契約中必備下列項目：

a) Date and Place
（日期，地點）

b) Purpose of the Contract （合約主旨）

c) Type of Goods
（貨品類型）

d) Prices （價格）

e) Offers （出價）

f) Orders （訂購量）

g) Letters of Credit
（信用狀）

l) Shipment （裝運）

m) Marine Insurance
（海險）

n) Claims （索賠）

o) Arbitration （仲裁）

p) Know-how License
（技術轉移授權）

q) Confidentiality
（極機密）

r) Term （條件）

j) Force Majeure   s) Proper Law
（不可抵抗的外力）   （專門法律）
k) Inspection（裝運須知） t) Signature（簽名）

訂立

較重要的契約，固然要有律師在場作見證人，但是一般情形，雙方訂立契約，就足以保障彼此利益了。最後，在訂立契約時，當認爲有加入某項的必要時，或有問題要提出來的時候，可以利用下列這些常用的句型：

I'd like to discuss the details of the contract.
（我想討論合約的細節。）

May I ask how you interpret this article?
（我能請問一下，您如何解釋這份條約呢？）

I'd like to talk about this point a little more.
（我想多談談這一點。）

Let's go over the details of this article again to avoid any confusion.
（讓我們一塊兒，把條約細節從頭檢查過，以免有任何混淆不清楚的問題。）

Won't you think over the terms of that article again?
（你不再考慮一次條款的條件嗎？）

We would like to insert an article on terminating this contract.
（我們想加入一項條款，來中止這項契約。）

We need a little more time to consider the contract.
（我們需要更多一點時間來考慮這份契約。）

LESSON 14

Shipment

MODEL DIALOGS ———————

1

A : (*On the phone*) ***Transportation Department***. Can I help you?

B : We have a cargo to be shipped to L.A. within this month. ***Can you provide space for our cargo***?

A : ***Thank you for your inquiry***. Would you tell me what your cargo is?

B : Our cargo is one box of medical machinery.

A : ***How much tonnage and measurement does your cargo have***?

B : It is about 700 kilograms and about 2 cubic meters of wooden box.

A : I see. We can provide space on the *Cupid* for you at the end of this month.

第十四課

裝船

對話範例 ─────────────

1

A：（電話中）運輸部。我能替你效勞嗎？

B：我們這個月有貨要用船運到洛杉磯，你能替我們的貨找到船位嗎？

A：謝謝您的查詢，能告訴我您的貨品是什麼嗎？

B：我們的貨是一箱醫療器材。

A：您的貨有幾噸重，規格是多少？

B：重約七百公斤，規格是兩立方公尺左右的木箱。

A：知道了。我們會替你把貨，在月底前用「邱比特號」運送。

---

cargo〔ˈkɑrgo〕*n.* 貨物

inquiry〔ɪnˈkwaɪrɪ〕*n.* 查詢

tonnage〔ˈtʌnɪdʒ〕*n.* 噸數

2

A : I'm not interested in just one order.

B : I understand what you mean. We'll inspect the shipment carefully.

A : That's what I wanted to say. We insist on first quality.

B : We guarantee that the quality of our goods will be the same as the original samples.

A : That's very important for both of us.

B : We have not had a single complaint about our quality.

3

A : When can you *make shipment* ?

B : We'll need at least 90 days after receipt of your L/C to make complete delivery of 50,000 sets.

A : Can't you make it 60 days ?

B : Then, we can make initial delivery of 30,000 sets in October, and the balance, 20,000 at the end of November.

A : If that's the best you can do, I agree.

B : Thank you very much. We shall try to speed up.

---

shipment〔'ʃɪpmənt〕*n.* 裝船

2

A：只有一張定單，我沒什麼興趣。（嫌生意太小，以退為進，提出要求）

B：我知道你的意思，我們裝運會小心檢查。

A：這正是我想說的，我們堅持品質第一。

B：我們保證貨品品質會和原先樣本一樣。

A：這對我們雙方都很重要。

B：我們從來沒有接到關於品質的抱怨。

3

A：你們何時可以裝船？

B：至少要在收到信用狀九十天以後，才能把五萬件貨品完全送達。

A：能不能改為六十天？

B：那麼，我們會在十月運第一批三萬件的貨，其餘的兩萬件，會在十一月底送達。

A：如果你已經盡力而為，我同意。

B：非常感謝，我們會盡量快一點。

---

complaint〔kəmˈplent〕*n*. 抱怨

4

A : *How soon can you make the delivery* ?
B : Within six weeks.
A : We can't lose the season. Please deliver two weeks
　　earlier.
B : Two weeks ? That's pretty tight.
A : Any chance we can get them sooner ?
B : All right. I'll see if I can make it.

SUPPLEMENTARY DIALOGS ———

A : Have you booked the space on any vessel yet ?
B : Yes, we'll send them by the *Ever Lucky* departing
　　Keelung on October 20.

A : How much is the freight from Keelung to New York?
B : $24 per ton of 40 cubic feet.

A : When are you going to get the backlog out ?
B : The remaining 500 dozen will be shipped on May 10.

A : What about insuring the shipment ?
B : I'm afraid you'll have to *take care of the insurance*.

---

vessel〔'vɛsḷ〕*n.* 船
freight〔fret〕*n.* 運費

4

A：你們要多久才會送貨？

B：六個星期以內。

A：我們不能錯過季節，請提早兩週送。

B：兩週？相當趕。

A：有沒有什麼辦法，我們可以快點拿到貨？

B：好吧，我看能不能辦得到。

補充會話 ————————————————

A：你是不是已經訂好船位了？

B：是的，十月二十號，由「長慶號」，從基隆出口。

A：從基隆到紐約的運費要多少？

B：一噸四十立方呎，美金24塊。

A：你們何時要把存貨出清？

B：剩下的五百打，會在五月十號裝船。

A：船運的保險怎麼算？

B：恐怕，保險費得由你們來付。

———————————————

backlog〔'bæk,lɔg , - ,lɑg〕*n.* 存貨
take care of the insurance 負擔保險費

BUSINESS ADVICE

"**SHIP**" 絕非僅意指裝船運貨而已，也包括利用陸上交通來運貨的 "發貨"，這一層意思。另外，"Shipment"包含有「裝貨」、「裝貨日期」、「裝好的貨」等多樣意義。當使用複數 "Shipment"，則意指將貨品分開發貨，也就是 "partial shipments"（分批裝貨）的意思。

> A： When can you ship the goods？
>
> （你什麼時候可以裝船運貨？）
>
> B： During March.
>
> （三月間。）
>
> A： Can't you ship earlier？
>
> （不能早點裝運嗎？）
>
> B： Well，the space is very scarce these days. So let's make it 'February/March'.
>
> （不過，最近船位很少。所以我們打算在二、三月間送。）

裝船 日期，一般而言，常以月份來表示，以上對話中所謂的 'February / March' 是指二月一號到三月三十一號都可以裝貨的意思。在這情形下，一般慣例是二月先裝一半的貨物，到了三月再裝上另一半的貨物，當然也可以作出如同下句一般

明確的指示：

> If you are in a hurry for goods, shall we ship one half during February and the rest during March?
> （如果你趕著要貨的話，我們能不能先在二月裝一半的貨，在三月再裝另一半的貨呢？）

● DELAY IN SHIPMENT

當裝貨延期（delay in shipment）的時候,隨著延期的時間長短，信用狀也同時要延長才行。這時候，買賣雙方可能會有這樣的對話：

A：Your goods will be ready by the end of the next month. So will you extend the credit?
（你的貨下個月底會到。所以，你要不要延長信用狀的期限呢？）

B：OK. But remember this is the last chance for you. We have already extended the credit twice. If you fail again, we'll have to cancel our order.
（好吧。但是記住，這是給你的最後一次機會了。我們信用狀已經延期兩次了。如果你們再無法如期到達，我們只好取消訂單了。）

裝貨 延遲也算一項違約行為，就算被取消也無話可說。不過，要是遇上像颱風之類的天災，或是遇到罷工、示威等不可抗拒的外力原因，只要能夠提出證明，證實是由於上述的某項原因，才導致裝貨延遲，就能避免被取消合約，而延長信用狀期限。不過，延長期限大約只有兩、三週，如果在此期限之內，仍無法完成裝貨的話，就算被取消，也無可奈何了。

LESSON 15

Claim Settlement

MODEL DIALOGS ─────────

1

A : We have a problem with your products.

B : What happened?

A : Some are heavily damaged *due to* loose packing. This is obviously your error.

B : We'll do everything we can to *straighten* things *out*.

A : That's not a concrete answer. You have to *answer for* any broken equipment.

B : We accept your complaint as being fair, but that's all we can say at this stage.

---

damaged〔ˈdæmɪdʒd〕*adj.* 損壞的
straighten out (使) 變直

第十五課
要求清償

對話範例

1

A：你們的產品有問題。

B：發生什麼事？

A：由於包裝鬆散，以致於有些貨物嚴重損壞。這分明是你們的錯。

B：我們已經盡力而為，把貨拉緊綁直。

A：這不是具體的答案。你們一定要對壞掉的儀器負責。

B：我們接受您合理的抱怨，但是目前我們只能這麼說。

---

answer for *sth.* 對某物負責

settlement〔'sɛtḷmənt〕*n.* 清償

2

A: (*On the phone*) The order we placed yesterday hasn't arrived yet.

B: Hold on a minute. I'll call the warehouse and check up on it.

A: Please do that.

B: We're sorry for the delay. It left there 30 minutes ago.

A: We're out of stock now.

B: I wish you wouldn't get so upset. You'll get your goods soon.

3

A: We offer a 10% reduction on the total shipment.

B: But, according to the survey report, the 10% was not entirely worthless.

A: But, as a matter of fact, our customer did not accept about 10% of the shipment, and we have not yet disposed of the rejected goods.

B: All right. Send the damaged pieces back to us, please.

A: Then, we'll meet you halfway. We'll bear 5%.

B: OK. We accept your proposal.

---

warehouse〔'wer,haʊs〕*n.* 倉庫
check up on *sth.* 檢查核對
out of stock 沒有存貨

2

A：（電話中）昨天訂的東西還沒到。

B：請等一會兒。我會打電話到倉庫，查核一下。

A：請便。

B：很抱歉就誤了，貨已經在三十分鐘前離開。

A：我們現在沒有存貨了。

B：希望您不要這麼心煩，很快您就能拿到貨。

3

A：整船貨物，我們要求少收百分之十的貨款。

B：但是根據檢查報告，這受損的百分之十並非全然一文不值。

A：可是，事實上，我們的顧客不會接受這百分之十的貨，而且我們還沒處理退貨呢。

B：好吧。請把損壞的組件退回來。

A：那麼，我們就和你妥協。我們會負擔百分之五的損失。

B：好，我們接受您的提議。

---

survey report　檢查報告

dispose of（ the rejected goods ）　處理（退貨）

meet sb. halfway　願意跟某人妥協

4

A : What's the trouble?

B : We have some unexpected production delays. Please extend the shipping date by two weeks.

A : No, we agreed already. I need the shipment on time.

B : But we won't be able to make it. I hope you understand we are proceeding as fast as we can.

A : All right, but this is the last time. Unless you can supply them by then, we have no alternative but to cancel the contract.

SUPPLEMENTARY DIALOGS ———

A : What's the problem?

B : The quality is not up to your usual standards.

A : What's the problem?

B : We've had complaints from our customer, and it's not very good.

A : We found that your last shipment was short of 10 units.

B : Oh, really? I'll send the missing units to you as soon as possible.

A : What we received was not what we ordered.

B : I'm sorry it happened. We'll send you the correct products immediately.

4

A：發生什麼麻煩了？

B：因為一些意外，我們出貨要晚些時候。請把船期挪後兩週。

A：不行，我們已經講好的。我要貨準時到達。

B：可是我們無能為力。希望您了解，我們已經盡力加快速度。

A：好吧，但這是最後一次了。除非你們能及時送到，否則我們沒有選擇餘地，只好取消契約。

補充會話 ────────────────

A：有什麼問題？

B：品質未達你們一般標準。

A：有什麼問題？

B：我們的顧客抱怨，東西不是很好。

A：我們發現，你們上一批貨少了十件。

B：喔，真的嗎？我會盡快把丟掉的件數補送給你。

A：我們收到的東西不是我們訂的。

B：很抱歉發生這種事。我們會把正確的產品立刻送過去給你。

BUSINESS ADVICE

交 易過程中，如果有輕微的不滿，不過是向對方抱怨（ complaint ）幾句罷了。但是所謂的 " claim " 就不同了, 乃是指「當有確實的損害發生，而要求對方賠償」的意思，而複數的 " claims " ，則有「賠償金」的意思。

會 提出 " claim " 的原因，追究起來，不外乎是貨品品質不良（ *inferior quality* ），或數量不足（ *shortage* ），還有貨物搞錯了（ *wrong* ），不然就是裝貨延期（ *delayed shipment* ），價格方面發生錯誤或對方未履行運貨的任務（ *non-delivery* ）等等各式各樣的原因，甚至還有所謂的 " *market claim* " ，意思是沒有任何理由，而提出的 claim。但是有一點必須記住，所謂 " claim" 一定是指「主張本身應有的權利」，絕非一般無理的要求。

◎ 如何處理Claim？

接到對方的 claim ，首先要立即進行調查, 如有發生錯誤，則立刻要向對方表明更正的態度。即使此時對方由於激動，而產生情緒化反應，所說的內容甚至已超出實情，我們由於理虧，言語及態度上，仍應保持謙恭，親切地對待對方。為了要壓抑對方強硬的態度，而要求自己說出像 "*We are surprised to hear that～*" 或 "*We regret～*" 之類的話，甚至一開始就得說 "*We are sorry～*" 等等，的確相當不容易，但如此可以表示我們已經認定接受對方的 claim ，否則,對於解決 claim,是非常不利的。

◎ 面對Claim時，常用的話

I'll look into it and try to get it corrected for you.

（我會檢查一下，想辦法替您改正過來。）

We cannot accept your claim.

（我們無法接受你們賠償的要求。）

This is surely our fault, we'll gladly change it for a new one.

（這當然是我們的錯，我們會非常樂意替您換一個新的。）

We shall be more careful not to repeat the same mistake.

（我們應該會更加小心，不要再犯同樣的錯誤。）

Well, I don't know if we can do it. Let me talk to our manager.

（我不知道我們到底能做什麼。讓我去和經理談。）

最後，"claim"如果能經由雙方商議，而獲得解決，當然是最好了。不過，萬一協議無法達成，而導致紛爭，就只好經由訴訟，以求得公平仲裁（**arbitrary**）。其實，不管是藉由任何途徑，任何技巧，任何方法，來獲得仲裁，還不如事先訂契約時，就確實訂立，明文規定，把"claim"防範於未然。

To Be Continued ......

PART 4

Entertaining a Buyer

接待買主

LESSON 16

A Business Lunch

MODEL DIALOGS ────────

1

A : It's almost noon. ***How about talking further over lunch***?

B : That would be fine.

A : Which do you prefer Korean, Japanese or American food?

B : I'd like to have Korean food.

A : Good.

B : Do you ***know of*** any good restaurants?

A : Yes. I know of a restaurant in the arcade in this building.

───────────

know of 知道

arcade〔ɑr'ked〕 *n*. 騎樓

第十六課

商業午餐

對話範例 ────────────────

1

A： 快中午了。何不一塊兒吃中飯，再進一步談呢？

B： 好呀。

A： 你喜歡吃韓菜，日本料理還是美式食物？

B： 我喜歡吃韓菜。

A： 好。

B： 你知道什麼好餐廳嗎？

A： 我知道這騎樓的一家餐廳不錯。

2

A : What would you like to have?

B : I don't know much about Chinese food.

A : Well, I suggest you try swallow's nest soup. It's one of our famous dishes.

B : It sounds like a big lunch! I'll try it.

A : OK. Shall we start with some beer?

B : No, not for me. But please go ahead, Mr. Kim.

A : *I better not*, then.

3

A : Have you ever tried any Chinese dishes?

B : No. I'm new in your country.

A : I'm sure you'll like eel noodles.

B : (*After lunch*) Thank you very much for the excellent Chinese dish. I really enjoyed it.

A : You seem to like Chinese food. How about having dinner at my house before you leave?

B : Really? I'd love to see a Chinese home.

---

try 〔 traɪ 〕 *v.* 嚐一嚐

I better not. 最好不要。(= *I had better not start with beer.*)

2

A： 你喜歡吃什麼？

B： 對中國菜我所知不多。

A： 那麼，建議你嚐嚐一品燕窩。那是一道有名的中國菜。

B： 聽起來好像一道大餐！我要嚐嚐。

A： 好的。要不要先喝點啤酒？

B： 不用，請自便，金先生。

A： 那麼，我最好也不喝。

3

A： 你吃過中國菜嗎？

B： 沒有吃過。我對你們國家很陌生。

A： 相信你會喜歡吃鱔魚麵。

B： （午餐後）謝謝你帶我去吃，這麼棒的中國菜。我真的吃得很開心。

A： 你似乎喜歡吃中國菜。離開前到我家吃晚飯如何？

B： 真的嗎？我好想去見識一下中國家庭。

eel noodle 鱔魚麵

4

A: Let me pay for mine.

B: No, I insist. *It's on me.*

A: Are you sure it's all right?

B: Of course. Anyway, I'm not the one who's *footing the bill*.

A: You mean your company is?

B: Yes. In Taiwan, it's a common practice to treat clients on the company's account.

A: Anyway, thank you.

SUPPLEMENTARY DIALOGS ————

A: How about lunch today?

B: I'm sorry, but I already have another appointment.

A: When is your lunch hour?

B: It's usually 12 to 1, but I'm flexible.

A: Could I see you Thursday morning?

B: I can always make time for you. I hope you stay longer and eat lunch with me.

A: Do you have time for lunch?

B: Sorry, I can't make it today. I've got a client.

It's on me. 我請客。(= *You're my quest.*)

foot the bill 付錢 (= *get the bill*)

4

A： 讓我自己付。
B： 萬萬不可。我請客。
A： 你確定沒關係嗎？
B： 當然。事實上，付錢的人又不是我。
A： 你是說公司會付？
B： 對。在台灣，請客戶報公費，是一般的慣例。
A： 不管怎麼說，還是謝謝你。

補充會話 ─────────────────────

A： 今天一塊兒吃中飯，如何？
B： 抱歉，我另外有約。

A： 你什麼時候吃午餐？
B： 通常是十二點到一點，有伸縮性。

A： 禮拜四早上可以見你嗎？
B： 我會替你安排時間。希望你待久一點，然後一塊兒吃中飯。

A： 有時間吃中飯嗎？
B： 抱歉，今天沒辦法。我要見個客戶。

---

client〔'klaɪənt〕*n*. 顧客
common practice 常見的慣例
flexible〔'flɛksəbl〕*adj*. 有伸縮性的

BUSINESS ADVICE

在 歐美，有一面吃午飯，一面洽談商務的慣例,這種午餐形式,
被稱爲 " business lunch "，也可稱爲 "working lunch"。
想要訂個商業午餐的約會，可以這麼說：

Would it be possible for us to have lunch tomorrow at
my hotel ?

（明天能到我住的旅館，一塊兒吃中飯嗎？）

Could we have lunch tomorrow to discuss the matter we
spoke of yesterday?

（明天能一塊兒吃中飯，談談昨天我們提到的那件事嗎？）

通 常商業午餐應要事先約好，但當會議太長，中午前不能結束
討論，偶而也會利用午餐時間，繼續磋商。因此，像這樣的
句型便很實用。

Would you like to | discuss / talk about | it over | lunch / a cup of coffee / a drink | ?

（你願意一邊 | 吃中飯 / 喝咖啡 / 喝飲料 | 一邊談事情嗎？）

商 談是 Business Lunch 是主要目的，不過時間最好是集中在
" 飯前酒 " 或 " 餐後甜點 " 的時間，比較得體合宜。

良 好的餐桌禮儀，可以表現修養、風範，讓您的客戶留下良好印象：

a. Don't make noise when you are eating or drinking.
（吃飯、喝湯的時候，不要發出聲音。）

b. Don't try to eat and talk.
（不要邊吃邊説話。）

c. Don't rush through your meal.
（不要狼吞虎嚥。）

d. Don't raise any plates or bowls when you eat.
（吃東西時，不要把碗盤拿起來。）

e. Don't pick your teeth at the table.
（不要在餐桌上剔牙。）

f. Don't use your handkerchief for napkin.
（不要用手帕當圍兜。）

g. Do make conversation.
（不要低頭猛吃，要真心交談。）

Lesson 17

At the Restaurant

MODEL DIALOGS ———————

1

A: (*On the phone*) Four Seasons Restaurant. May I help you?

B: Yes. I'd like to **make a reservation for** dinner tomorrow.

A: I see. What time will you come, sir?

B: Around 7.

A: May I have your name, please?

B: Mike Chen.

A: **How many will be in your party?**

B: Three. I'd prefer a table by the window.

---

party〔'pɑrtɪ〕 *n.* 餐會

第十七課

在餐廳中

對話範例 ————————————

1

A：（電話中）四季餐廳。我能替您效勞嗎？
B：我想預定明天晚餐的座位。
A：喔，先生，您什麼時候會到呢？
B：大約七點左右。
A：請問大名？
B：陳邁克。
A：總共有多少人？
B：三個人。我喜歡靠窗戶的桌子。

2

A : Do you have *a table for two*?

B : Do you have a reservation?

A : No.

B : I'm sorry, but there're no tables available right now.

A : How long will it be?

B : I'm not sure.... In about 20 minutes? Would you like to wait in the bar?

A : Fine. Please call us when you have a table.

3

A : May I take your order, sir?

B : Yes. This gentleman will have the beef stew, and I'll have the sirloin steak.

A : Yes, sir. And how would you like your beef?

B : Well-done, please.

A : (*Turning to C*) How about you, sir?

C : Medium-rare, please.

A : Yes, sir. Would you like a drink first with your meal?

B : Why don't we have cocktails?

---

table for two 兩個人的桌位   sirloin〔ˈsɝlɔɪn〕*n.* 牛腰肉

2

A： 有兩個人的桌位嗎？

B： 請問有沒有訂位？

A： 沒有。

B： 很抱歉，現在沒有桌位。

A： 那要等多久呢？

B： 我不確定。……大概要二十分鐘吧。您願意在吧台等嗎？

A： 好的。有桌位時，請叫我們。

3

A： 先生，請問要點什麼？

B： 這位先生要燉牛肉，我要牛腰肉牛排。

A： 好的，先生。請問您要幾分熟的牛肉？

B： 請給我全熟的。

A： （問 C ）那麼，先生您呢？

C： 請給我五分熟的。

A： 是的，先生。飯前要不要先來杯飲料？

B： 何不來杯雞尾酒？

---

well-done〔ˈwɛlˈdʌn〕*adj.* 全熟的

4

A : This was a splendid meal. I really enjoyed it.

B : I'm glad you liked it. Will you have a cognac to **round off** the meal?

A : I don't mind if I do.

B : Waiter, show me the cognac list.

C : Yes, sir.

SUPPLEMENTARY DIALOGS ——

A : What will you have, sir?

B : Just a moment, please. I haven't decided yet.

A : What do you recommend?

B : Our specialty for the day is roast duck.

A : What would you like for dessert?

B : I'll skip the dessert.

A : This is not what I ordered.

B : I'm sorry, sir.

---

splendid〔'splɛndɪd〕 *adj.* 極佳的（= *satisfactory*〔,sætɪs-'fæktərɪ〕 *adj.* 令人滿意的）

cognac〔'konjæk〕 *n.* 法國 *Cognac* 所產的白蘭地酒

round off 使其圓滿結束

4

A：這頓飯真令人滿意。我吃得真開心。
B：很高興你喜歡。飯後要不要來杯白蘭地？
A：好啊！
B：服務生，給我看看白蘭地的目錄。
C：好的，先生。

補充會話 ─────────────

A：先生，請問要吃什麼？
B：請稍待一會兒，我還沒決定。

A：你會推薦那道菜呢？
B：我們今天的特餐是烤鴨。

A：請問你想吃什麼飯後甜點？
B：我不吃甜點。

A：這不是我點的東西。
B：先生，對不起。

---

specialty〔ˈspɛʃəltɪ〕*n.* 特製品
skip〔skɪp〕*v.* 去掉；遺漏

BUSINESS ADVICE

在 飯店招待商業客戶，必須在事先一、兩天就預約好。尤其是星期五、六晚餐，預約最好在週一就確定好。要在飯店預訂桌位，可以這麼說：

I'd like to reserve a table for 4 at 7 tomorrow evening.
（明天晚上七點，我想訂四人一桌的位子。）

Do you have a table for 2 at 6 o'clock on Friday?
（你們星期五六點鐘，還有沒有兩個人的桌位？）

當 天，應比客戶早到，來迎接客戶，才不算失禮。縱使已事先預約好，還要知會一下飯店經理（Maître d'hotel），拜託他好好招呼客戶，這是必備的程序。

大 衣儘量寄放在衣物間（check room），如果有女秘書及夫人隨行的話，一般習慣把女性的大衣掛在自己椅子後面。詢問對方是否需要幫忙託放大衣，可以說：

May I check your coat?
（要我幫你寄放外套嗎？）

用餐後，再替客戶取回大衣。

在台灣，一般太太都不過問丈夫的工作；而在歐美，太太不但非常關心丈夫的工作事業，有時還肩負協助的角色，所以與外國客戶會面，別儘顧和先生討論，而冷落了客戶的太太。

◎ 大風吹！猜猜看，你該坐那個位子？

進餐廳，主人儘可能最後坐下，如果只接待一個人，就請他坐在右邊；有兩個人，就請他們分坐在您的兩側，以便交談。

上座一般是請長者和女士坐，而上座隨飯店擺設而少有差異，通常是指靠邊的位子，或是視野最好的位子。

有些飯店的服務費，已一併包含在餐費之中，不必另付。否則，給侍者的小費，約當餐費的 10～15％，較為適當。

Lesson 18

Going to a Bar

MODEL DIALOGS ————————

1

A : I know you are very busy in Taipei, but I'd like to take you out for dinner.

B : It would be a pleasure.

A : How about tomorrow night?

B : Fine. Shall we meet at your office?

A : No, I'll pick you up at your hotel at 6, *if that's convenient for you*.

B : Good, I'll be ready then.

————————

if that is convenient for you 如果你方便的話

第十八課

去酒吧

對話範例

1

A：我知道你在台北很忙，不過我想帶你出去吃晚餐。

B：那是我的榮幸。

A：明天晚上如何？

B：好呀。我們在你辦公室碰頭嗎？

A：不。如果你方便的話，六點我會到你住的旅館接你。

B：好的，到時候我會在那兒等你。

2

A : What would you like to drink, sir?

B : I'll have a whisky.

A : And what would be yours?

C : I'll have the same.

A : How about something to *go with* the drink?

B : Cheese and peanuts, please.

A : Yes, sir.

C : This is a very nice restaurant.

B : Yes.　I often come here because of its quiet atmosphere.

3

A : This is one of the famous night clubs in Taipei.

B : I've never been to an exciting place like this.

A : The show here is really something to see.

B : It sounds great.

A : Well, cheers!　To your health!

B : Cheers!... Ah, that's better.

A : It's gone.　Let me refill your glass.

B : Thanks, that's plenty.

---

go with 配合　　atmosphere〔'ætməs,fɪr〕 *n.* 氣氛

2

A： 先生，請問你想喝點什麼？

B： 給我一杯威士忌。

A： 那麼先生你呢？

C： 一樣。

A： 要不要來點下酒的東西？

B： 請來點乳酪和花生。

A： 好的，先生。

C： 這是家非常好的餐廳。

B： 是呀，因為它氣氛安靜，所以我常到這兒。

3

A： 這是家台北知名的夜總會。

B： 我從來沒到過像這裏這麼刺激的地方。

A： 這裏的表演真的頗有看頭。

B： 聽起來很棒嘛。

A： 好，乾杯！祝你健康。

B： 乾杯。……啊，好多了。

A： 喝完了，讓我再替你倒滿。

B： 謝謝，已經很多了。

4

A : Did I drink! I'm afraid I must go.

B : Oh, don't go yet. Let me take you to just one more place for a few more drinks.

A : If you insist.

B : Waiter, *get* me *the bill*, please.

A : No. I'll *take care of* this.

B : *No way*! You're my guest tonight.

A : OK. Next time I'll treat.

SUPPLEMENTARY DIALOGS ——

A : Would you *care for* a drink?

B : I'm sorry, but I'm busy today. May I take a *rain check*?

A : Let's toast! To your success!

B : Thank you. To your success, too.

A : How about another drink?

B : Oh, I couldn't drink another sip!

A : Allow me to get the bill.

B : No, no. This round's on me.

If you insist. 如果你堅持的話 。

get the bill 買單 ; 付帳　　*take care of* 處理 ; 負責

No way! 不行 !

4

A：我眞的喝了不少！恐怕我得走了。

B：喔，別走嘛。讓我再帶你到另一個地方，多喝兩杯。

A：如果你堅持的話。

B：服務生，請買單。

A：不，我來付。

B：不行！今晚你是客人。

A：好吧，下次我請客。

補充會話 ————————————

A：你想喝一杯嗎？

B：抱歉，我今天很忙。改天好嗎？

A：敬你一杯酒，祝你成功！

B：謝謝。也祝你成功。

A：要不要再喝一杯？

B：喔，我一口也喝不下去了。

A：讓我付帳。

B：不，不。這頓歸我請。

———————————————

You're my quest tonight. 今晚你是我的客人。

care for 喜歡　　*rain check* 雙方同意某方延遲履行承諾

sip〔sɪp〕*n.* 啜

BUSINESS ADVICE

勸 客戶喝酒可以說：

Would you want something to drink ?
（你要不要喝點什麼？）

也可以用比較正式而婉轉的口氣問：

Would you like something to drink ?
Would you care for something to drink ?

替 客戶倒酒時，可以用：" Say when ? "，來詢問對方，要倒到什麼程度。

如果你接受別人斟酒，覺得份量夠了，可以簡單地告訴對方：

" Yes, thank you. "

倒 雞尾酒威士忌（ Scotch and Water ）時，先說" Say when "，再倒威士忌酒，然後問" Say when "，再加水，最後要加冰塊時，才問：

" Would you care for some ice ? "

如果要加冰塊，就說：" Yes, please. "，只說" Yes. "是很不禮貌的。

如果不要加冰塊，就說："No, thank you."

乾杯要歡呼時候，歡呼用詞隨聚會性質而異。

⇨ 親友、同事輕鬆歡聚時，可以說：

Cheers！或 Prosit！

To Your good health！

Here's to your trip！

⇨ 在正式場合，（如：婚禮），則可使用下列語句：

Please join me in a toast to Mary and John.

（請跟我一起，向瑪麗和約翰敬酒。）

Now, Ladies and Gentlmen, I'd like to ask you to
join me in drinking a toast to our guests from London.

（現在，各位先生，各位女士，我想請你們和我一起，向
我們從倫敦來的客人敬酒。）

So, let us drink a toast to our good friend, Mr. Johnson.

（因此，讓我們一起，敬我們的好朋友，強森先生一杯。）

Ladies and Gentlemen, let us drink to the long life
and prosperity, and happiness of Bride and Groom.

（各位女士，各位先生，讓我們一起敬新郎和新娘，祝他
們長壽、富貴和快樂！）

Now, Ladies and Gentlemen, will you stand up and
drink a toast to the health and happiness of Mary and
John？

（現在，各位女士，各位先生，您是不是願意起立，敬瑪
麗和約翰一杯，祝他們健康快樂？）

Lesson 19

Shopping and Sightseeing

MODEL DIALOGS ─────────────

1

A : Shall we do some shopping this afternoon?

B : That sounds like a good idea.

A : Where would you like to go?

B : I'd like to *leave* that *up to* you.

A : I see. Are you looking for something in particular?

B : Yes. I want to buy some souvenirs for my family.

A : OK. I'll get the car.

─────────────

leave sth. (*up*) *to sb.* 交由某人負責某事

第十九課

購物與觀光

對話範例

1

A：今天下午我們去逛逛街，好嗎？

B：這主意聽起來不錯。

A：想去那裏？

B：我想，由你決定。

A：哦。你是不是在找什麼特別的東西？

B：是啊，我想給家人買點紀念品。

A：好的，我去開車。

---

souvenir〔'suvə,nɪr〕*n.* 紀念品

2

A： Is there something special you're looking for?

B： Yes. I'm interested in Chinese handcrafts.

A： Then, let's start with Yinko. There are a lot of small stores *specializing in* them in that area.

B： (*Upon arriving Yinko*) Why don't we have a look in this shop?

A： All right.

B： Where does this exquisite horse come from?

A： It's a Táng Dynasty style, but a modern version.

3

A： Would you like to *stop for* a cup of coffee or something?

B： I'd love to.

A： (*At a coffee shop*) What would you like?

B： Coffee would be fine.

A： You bought nice things, especially the doll.

B： Yes. My daughter will love it.

A： I'm sure she will.

---

specialize in 專門

2

A：你是不是要找什麼特別的東西？

B：是啊，我對中國民間手工藝，很感興趣。

A：那麼，我們從鶯歌開始。那裏有很多專門賣這些東西的小店。

B：（到鶯歌）何不進去這家店瞧瞧？

A：好啊。

B：這個精緻的馬型雕像是哪裏來的？

A：它叫唐三彩，不過是現代仿製品。

3

A：要不要停下來喝杯咖啡或什麼？

B：我很樂意。

A：（在咖啡店）你想喝什麼？

B：咖啡就可以了。

A：你買了好東西，尤其是這個洋娃娃。

B：是啊，我女兒會喜歡。

A：我相信她一定會喜歡。

---

exquisite〔'ekskwɪzɪt〕*adj.* 精緻的
stop for 停下來做某事

4

A： You must be tired.

B： Not really.　I've seen so much that I haven't had time to think about it.

A： Anyway, I hope you enjoyed yourself today.

B： I sure did.　Thank you for all you've done for me.

A： You're welcome. Would you like to go back to the hotel？

SUPPLEMENTARY DIALOGS ———

A： I'm going to try to do some shopping this afternoon.

B： Well, if you like, I'll come along with you.

A： If you'd like, I can show you around the city.

B： Oh, I'd like to.

A： How much does it cost？

B： He says it is $1,100 N.T. *tax free*.　That's about $40 at today's *exchange rate*.

A： Why don't we try some other places ？

B： That's a good idea.

---

　　tax free 已付稅的　　　*exchange rate* 兌換率

4

A：你一定累了。

B：倒沒有真的很累。我看了那麼多東西，以致於沒空想到累不累。

A：不管怎麼說，希望你今天玩得很開心。

B：當然囉。謝謝你幫的忙。

A：不客氣。你要回旅館了嗎？

補充會話

A：今天下午我想去買東西。

B：好的，如果你喜歡，我會陪你去。

A：如果你願意，我可以帶你到城裏四處看看。

B：喔，我喜歡。

A：這多少錢呢？

B：他說連同稅金是台幣一千一。按今天滙率大概是美金四十元。

A：何不多問幾家店呢？

B：好主意。

BUSINESS ADVICE

陪客戶購物、逛街時，常用的句型有以下這幾句：

● 建議與邀請

How about some shopping with me tomorrow？
（明天何不跟我一塊兒買東西？）

I'd like to take you to sightseeing.
（我想帶你去觀光。）

I'd recommend the afternoon tour of the city.
（我建議下午到城裏，四處看看。）

● 詢問對方的意見

In what are you particularly interested in Taipei？
（你對台北的什麼事物，特別感興趣？）

Is there any place you'd particularly like to go？
（你特別想去那裏？）

Are you looking for anything specific？
Is there anything special you're looking for？
（您在找什麼特別的東西嗎？）

提個好點子！

Shall we start with one of the leading department stores?
（我們從一家第一流的百貨公司，開始參觀，好不好？）

Why don't we have a look around in this store?
（我們何不到這家店四處看看？）

Let's look around in this store.
（讓我們到這家店，四處看看。）

I think it's too expensive. Why don't we
look around a little more before you decide?
（我覺得它太貴了。我們在你決定之前，何
不先四處多看看呢？）

You've bought me some really nice things.
（你已經買給我一些，非常好的東西。）

I'm sorry, but taking picture is not al-
lowed here.
（抱歉，這裡不准照相。）

I hope you enjoyed the day.
（我希望你今天玩得開心。）

Lesson 20

Dinner in an American Home

MODEL DIALOGS ————————

1

A : Good evening, Mr. Benson. ***Thanks for your invitation.***

B : Come in. Let me take your coat.

A : Thank you.

B : Susan, I'd like you to meet Mr. Lin from Taiwan.
Mr. Lin, this is my wife, Susan.

A : How do you do, Mrs. Benson. I'm glad to meet you.

C : How do you do, Mr. Lin? I'm glad you could come.

A : I've brought you some flowers. I hope you like
them.

C : Oh, they're lovely. Thank you.

第二十課

在美式家庭吃晚餐

對話範例 ─────────

1

A：晚安，班森先生。謝謝您的邀請。

B：請進。讓我替你拿外套。

A：謝謝。

B：蘇珊，我要你見見台灣來的林先生。林先生，這是內人蘇珊。

A：你好，班森太太。很高興認識你。

C：你好，林先生。很高興你能來。

A：我給你買了些花，希望你喜歡。

C：喔，花好可愛啊。謝謝你。

2

A： Please go ahead, Mr. Lin.

B： Thank you, I will. Mmm, everything looks very delicious.

A： I hope you like tomato soup.

B： Yes, it's my favorite. Would you pass the pepper?

A： Here you are.

B： Thank you. It's just delicious!

A： I'm glad you enjoy it. It's one of my wife's specialties.

3

A： Would you like some more meat?

B： No, thank you. I've already had enough.

A： Would you like to have tea or coffee?

B： Coffee, please.

A： Cream and sugar?

B： Yes, please. (*After a couple of hours*) Oh, *I didn't realize it was this late.* I must say good-bye.

A： Can't you stay a little longer?

B： No. I'd better be going. Thank you very much for the delicious dinner.

---

favorite 〔ˈfevə,rɪt〕 *n.* 最喜歡的事物

2

A：林先生，請用。

B：謝謝你，我自己來。嗯，每樣菜看起來都非常美味。

A：希望你喜歡蕃茄湯。

B：是的，那是我最愛吃的。請把胡椒傳過來，好嗎？

A：胡椒給你。

B：謝謝你。美味極了。

A：很高興你吃得開心。這是我太太的一道拿手菜。

3

A：要不要多吃點肉？

B：不，謝謝。我已經吃飽了。

A：要不要來杯茶，或者是咖啡？

B：請給我杯咖啡。

A：要不要加奶精和糖？

B：好的，謝謝。（過了幾小時）噢，我不知道已經這麼晚了。
我得說再見了。

A：不能待久一點嗎？

B：恐怕不行。我想最好告辭了。非常謝謝您美味的晚餐招待。

---

pepper〔ˋpɛpɚ〕*n.* 胡椒

4

A： I've had a very nice time.

B： We've also enjoyed your visit. I hope the meal was to your liking.

A： The dinner was wonderful.

B： I'm happy to hear that.

A： The next time you're in Taipei, I want to be an equally good host.

B： I'll be looking forward to it. *Take care on your way home.*

SUPPLEMENTARY DIALOGS——

A： I'm afraid I won't be in time due to a traffic jam. Please start dinner without waiting for me.

B： That's too bad. We'll wait till you arrive.

A： May I show you around my house?

B： Yes, please. You have a lovely home.

A： I'd like to have you over to my place in the near future.

B： I'll look forward to it.

A： It's getting late. I have to run along.

B： So soon? It's still early.

---

liking〔'laɪkɪŋ〕*n.* 胃口   host〔host〕*n.* 主人
take care on one's way home 回家路上當心

4

A： 我玩得很開心。

B： 我們也很高興您能來訪。希望這頓飯合您的胃口。

A： 晚餐很棒。

B： 聽到你這麼說,我很高興。

A： 下次你來台北,我也要做一個好主人。

B： 我早已迫不及待了。回家路上小心。

補充會話

A： 由於交通阻塞,恐怕我無法及時趕到。請開始用餐,不用等
我了。

B： 太糟了。我們會等到你來。

A： 我可以帶你在我家四處看看嗎?

B： 請。……你家非常可愛。

A： 希望最近請你到我那兒去。

B： 我會期待你的邀請。

A： 時間晚了,我得走了。

B： 這麼快?還早嘛。

---

run along 出發

BUSINESS ADVICE

晚上被邀請到別人家中作客，在歐美習慣上，要爲女主人準備一份簡單的禮物，叫做"hostess gift"（女主人的禮物），這類禮物通常是一些室內飾品，或廚房用品，以高貴不貴爲最佳！

在這種非正式的晚宴中，向客人介紹自己的太太時，通常只稱其名，不稱其姓。如：

I'd like to introduce you to my wife, Susan.
（我想介紹你給我太太蘇珊認識。）

EAST vs WEST

國人在家接待客人，往往說：「寒舍簡陋，敬請見諒。」之類的話，而歐美人士則認爲，他們的家雖非超級豪華住宅，卻是世界上最美好的地方。因此，自然地，在招待客人時，往往會問：

May I show you my home?
（容我向你展覽我的家！）

當我們受邀到別人家參觀，應該不吝讚揚。你可以說：

You have a lovely home.
（你家很可愛！）

...at a beautiful lamp!

（好漂亮的燈！）

This is a very interesting picture.

（這是幅非常有意思的圖畫。）

獲得讚美的主人，便會非常開心。

⬡ TABLE MANNERS

到別人家中作客，如果桌上的菜很好吃，應不吝讚揚。我們可以說：

This salad is very good.

（沙拉很好吃。）

This meat is very delicious.

（肉很美味。）

This dressing is very tasty.

（這調味料很美味。）

主婦由於手藝獲得肯定，定會感到十分高興。

*　　　　*　　　　*　　　　*

在歐美，女主人未上桌前，不可開動。當主人把餐巾放在膝上時，客人才可以跟著做；當女主人用手指向食物，並說："Please help yourself."（請自己來,不要客氣。）的時候，才表示可以開動。這是絕不能忽略的禮儀。

禮貌上，接受招待的人，隔天必須親筆寫封簡單的謝函，或用一束鮮花，來表示謝意，也可以用回請的方式來答謝對方。

Lesson 21

Attending a Party

MODEL DIALOGS ──────────

1

A : (*On the phone*) I'm giving a cocktail party. Could you join us?

B : Thank you. I'd be pleased to go.

A : Good. I'll be expecting you. The party will start next Friday at 4.

B : Where will it be?

A : At the Hotel Silla. The party will be very informal, so I'm sure you will *feel* quite *at home*.

---

informal 〔 ɪnˈfɔrml̩ 〕 *adj.* 非正式的

第二十一課

參加宴會

對話範例————————————

1

A：（電話中）我要舉行雞尾酒會，你能來參加嗎？

B：謝謝你。我很樂意前往。

A：好，酒會將在下週五四點舉行，到時候我會等你。

B：地點是哪裏？

A：希拉旅館。這不是正式酒會，所以我確信你會覺得相當自在。

2

A : May I have your invitation card, sir?

B : Yes, here it is. The party begins at 7?

A : Yes, sir. Quite a few guests have arrived already.

B : And where is the *check room*?

A : It's right around the corner. And the party will be held in the main banquet hall.

B : I see. Thank you.

3

A : Good evening, Mr. Harris. Thank you for inviting me.

B : You're quite welcome. I'm so glad you could come.

A : I'm sure this will be one of my happiest experience during my stay in your country.

B : Thank you. I hope you will enjoy the evening.

A : Thanks a lot.

---

invitation card 邀請卡

check room 衣帽間 (= *cloak room*)

2

A：先生，請讓我看看您的邀請卡。
B：在這兒。酒會七點開始嗎？
A：是的，先生，已經有好幾位客人到了。
B：衣帽間在那兒？
A：就在轉角那邊。酒會將在大宴會廳舉行。
B：知道了，謝謝你。

3

A：晚安，哈瑞斯先生。謝謝你邀請我。
B：不客氣。好高興你能來。
A：我相信，這會是我在貴國期間，最快樂的經驗。
B：謝謝。希望你今晚玩得開心。
A：非常謝謝。

---

banquet〔ˋbæŋkwɪt〕*n.* 宴會

4

A: Nice party, isn't it?

B: Yes, it sure is.

A: I don't think we've met. My name is Henry Young. I'm with Great Electronics Corp..

B: How do you do? I'm William Jones. I *deal in* electric appliances. Care for a drink?

A: Oh, yes. You seem very fit, do you jog or something?

B: Yes, I've been running 5 kilometers every morning before going to work.

SUPPLEMENTARY DIALOGS——

A: Can you join us for dinner next Friday?

B: Thank you for asking me, but I've got another appointment that evening.

A: I just want to say thanks for the party last night.

B: I'm glad you came. Did you enjoy it?

A: Thanks for that *going-away party* last night.

B: Don't mention it. We'll always miss doing business with you.

A: Why didn't you come last night?

B: I really meant to go, but I just couldn't get away.

---

deal in 買賣（= *buy or sell something*）

4

A：很棒的酒會，對不對？

B：當然是的。

A：我想我們沒見過面吧。我是楊亨利。我服務於濟業電子。

B：你好。我是威廉瓊斯。我從事電氣用品買賣。想喝一杯嗎？

A：喔，好呀。你身材很好。你是不是慢跑或做其他運動？

B：是的，每天早上上班前，我都跑五公里。

補充會話 ─────────────────

A：下星期五能和我們一塊兒晚餐嗎？

B：謝謝你的邀請，不過那天晚上，我已經另外有約了。

A：我只是要為昨晚的酒會向你道謝。

B：你來了我很開心。你玩得高興嗎？

A：謝謝昨晚的歡送酒會。

B：不必客氣。我們會永遠懷念和你做生意的情形。

A：昨晚為什麼沒來呢？

B：我真的想去，但就是無法抽身。

---

appliance〔əˊplaɪəns〕*n*. 電器用具

BUSINESS ADVICE

舉行雞尾酒會或晚宴，邀請函要提前兩週寄發，這段到設宴日的空檔時間，叫做 "*lead time*"。有些邀請函上會寫著 *R.S.V.P.*，這是法文 "*Répondez S'il vous plaît.*" 的縮寫，意思是希望對方接到邀請函後，能回信告知是否參加。"*Please reply.*" 也能表達同樣的意思。

接到邀請卡，不論參加與否，都要**親筆回信**，以示慎重。

⇨表示願意參加時，可以寫如下的回條：

Thank you for the invitation on Tuesday, September 10, at 8:00 p.m. I'll be very happy to come.
（謝謝你邀請我參加九月十號星期二，晚上八點的酒會。我樂意前往。）

⇨萬一無法參加，也要回信婉轉告知理由：

I am very sorry that I cannot accept your invitation on Tuesday, September 10, because....
（很遺憾不能接受您的邀請，參加九月十號星期二的酒會，因為～）

在正式的宴會中，穿著不得體，會顯得失禮，最好按請柬上的指示穿著赴宴。

"white tie" ⇨ 穿燕尾服（tail coat）

"black tie"及"formal" ⇨ 穿無尾的半正式禮服（tuxe-do），打黑色蝴蝶結。

到 達宴會場所，拿飲料之前，必須先和主人（host）及貴賓（quests of honor）打招呼：

Thank you very much for inviting me.
（非常感謝你邀請我。）

I appreciate your hospitality.
（感激您的殷勤款待。）

It's so nice of you to invite me this evening.
（你今晚邀請我參加，真是太好了。）

參加宴會者應積極設法加入別人的談話，以維持融洽的氣氛。如果只是一個人呆呆地站在角落，或是只顧著吃，都是很不禮貌的行為。

THE END

宴會結束，離去前，應向主人說些感謝的話，順便向主人道別。

你可以這麼說：

I really enjoyed the party this evening.
（今晚的酒會，我玩得很開心。）

I've really enjoyed myself thoroughly.
（我真的玩得很盡興。）

To Be Continued ......

PART 5

Going Overseas
海外出差

Lesson 22

Making an appointment

MODEL DIALOGS ────────────

1

A: (*On the phone*) Tomorrow I'll be coming on a two week business trip to the United States. I'd like to **drop in** on you Friday morning.

B: I'm sorry, but I'm all **booked up** this week. How about next week?

A: Can we make it next Monday, then?

B: What time are you thinking of?

A: Is 11 o'clock all right with you?

B: That'll be fine with me.

─────────────────────

drop in 順道拜訪

第二十二課

訂約會

對話範例

1

A：（電話中）明天我要到美國，做為期兩週的商務旅行。星期五早上想順道去拜訪你。

B：抱歉，我整個禮拜時間都排滿了。下個星期如何？

A：那麼，我們約下星期一，好嗎？

B：你想什麼時間合適呢？

A：十一點，你可以嗎？

B：沒問題。

---

book up 預約已滿

2

A: (*On the phone*) Hello. This is Henry Young.

B: Hi, Mr. Young. When did you arrive?

A: I just got here myself. I brought the samples you inquired about.

B: Glad to know you're back. When would you like to come?

A: How about tomorrow morning at 10?

B: Suits me fine.

A: I'll see you then.

3

A: (*On the phone*) Mr. Smith's secretary speaking.

B: May I speak to Mr. Smith, please?

A: I'm sorry he's out right now. May I ask who's calling?

B: This is Henry Young of Great Electronic Corp.. I'd like to make an appointment with him tomorrow.

A: May I ask what your business is?

B: I'd like to introduce our products.

A: I see. What time are you planning to come?

B: Three o'clock would be fine. Is that convenient for him?

2

A：（電話中）喂。我是楊亨利。

B：嗨，楊先生。你什麼時候到的？

A：我剛到。我帶來了你要的樣本。

B：很高興知道你回來了。你想什麼時候過來呢？

A：明天早上十點，如何？

B：我可以。

A：到時候見。

3

A：（電話中）我是史密斯先生的秘書。

B：請接史密斯先生，謝謝。

A：抱歉，他剛剛出去了。請問大名？

B：我是濟業電子的楊亨利。我想約他明天見面。

A：請問有什麼事嗎？

B：我想介紹我們公司的產品。

A：原來如此。你打算什麼時候來呢？

B：三點。史密斯先生方便嗎？

4

A : (*On the phone*) Mr. Smith's secretary speaking.

B : Good morning. This is Henry Young.

A : Oh! Good morning, Mr. Young.

B : I'm just calling to confirm my appointment with Mr. Smith for this afternoon.

A : Is it at 3 p.m.?

B : That's right.

A : He is expecting you at 3.

B : Fine. Thank you.

SUPPLEMENTARY DIALOGS ———

A : Let's **make a date**. How about 10 in the morning on Tuesday?

B : That's fine with me.

A : Can you come at two o'clock?

B : Sorry, I have an important meeting at 2:30. Can you make it at 4?

A : I wonder if I could change my appointment from 10:30 to 3:00 this afternoon?

B : No problem at all.

A : Something has come up. I won't be able to make it today.

B : That's quite all right. I know you are busy.

4

A：（電話中）我是史密斯先生的秘書。

B：早安，我是楊亨利。

A：喔，楊先生，您早。

B：我只是打個電話過來，確定一下今天下午和史密斯先生的約會。

A：是今天下午三點鐘嗎？

B：沒錯。

A：他三點會等你來。

B：好的，謝謝。

補充會話 ─────────────

A：約個時間吧。星期二早上十點，如何？

B：我沒問題。

A：你二點能來嗎？

B：抱歉，我兩點半有個重要的會。你四點能來嗎？

A：不知道可不可以把約會時間，從上午十點半改到下午三點？

B：沒有問題。

A：發生了點事情。我今天沒辦法來赴約。

B：沒關係，我知道你很忙。

BUSINESS ADVICE

美國人和別人見面前，習慣先以電話預約，當然業務上的拜訪，也要事先預約。預約，通常是先打電話到對方辦公室，再由對方秘書安排會面時間，此時不一定要和本人通話。

在美國，來訪面談的時間長短，秘書可以全權決定，他是老板的左右手，有很大的影響力，因此和秘書通電話，要特別注意禮貌，自我介紹時，必須清楚報上**自己姓名、所屬公司**，以及**訪談目的**。如：

My name is David Wang. I am with Acer Industrial Corp..
（我是王大衛，服務於宏碁電腦。）

I'd like to speak to him about our new products.
（我想跟他談談，我們的新產品。）

Mr. Brown suggested that I contact Mr. Smith.
（布朗先生建議我應該跟史密斯先生連絡。）

預約的要訣

1. 訂見面的時候，**不要說**：" Any time will be fine. "

2. 要把自己方便的時間講明，如：

I can come on Thursday around 2 p.m.. Is that convenient for him?

（我星期四兩點左右能來，那時候他有空嗎？）

3. 有急事不能赴會，必須取消時，要事先儘早聯絡對方，簡述原因，延期再見。

   I am sorry to have to ask this favor, but would it be possible for me to change my appointment from 2:00 to 4:00 this afternoon.

   （抱歉，請問能不能幫個忙，可不可能把約會，從兩點延到四點？）

4. 如果認為沒有再見面的必要，還是不可忽略應有的禮節，記得感謝對方撥空接見，並取得對方諒解，取消約會。你可以說：

   Thank you for you time.

   （謝謝你撥空接見。）

   It was pleasure talking to you.

   （跟你談話，很愉快。）

Lesson 23

At the Airport

MODEL DIALOGS

1

Ladies and Gentlemen. We're making a final approach to Kennedy Airport of New York. Please make sure that your seat belt is securely fastened and observe NO SMOKING until the plane comes to a complete stop at the terminal gate. Also, please put your table and seat back to a full upright and locked position. Thank you.

A : Fasten your seat belt, please. We're beginning to make our descent into the airport.

B : I see. What's the time difference between Taipei and New York?

A : Taipei is 16 hours ahead of us, sir.

B : Then New York time is 2:45 now.

A : Yes, sir.

第二十三課

機場

對話範例

1

各位女士，各位先生。我們就要在紐約的甘迺迪機場降落了。請確實繫好您的安全帶，在飛機停妥前，請勿抽煙。同時，請將您的桌椅拉直並且鎖定。謝謝。

A：請繫緊您的安全帶，我們要降落到機場了。

B：知道了。台北和紐約時差多少？

A：台北比我們早十六個小時。

B：那麼現在紐約當地時間是二點四十五分了。

A：是的，先生。

---

descent〔dɪ'sɛnt〕 *n.* 降落

terminal〔'tɝmənḷ〕 *n.* 機場候機處

time difference 時差

2

A: May I see your passport, please?
B: Here you are.
A: How long do you plan to stay?
B: For two weeks.
A: What's the purpose of your visit?
B: I'm here on a business trip.
A: I see. Where are you going to stay?
B: At the Hilton Hotel.
A: Fine. Have a nice stay in America.

3

A: May I see your customs declaration?
B: Here it is.
A: Do you have anything to declare?
B: No. All I have are personal things.
A: Do you mind opening your suitcase, please?
B: Not at all.
A: What's in this package?
B: These are business samples.
A: Do you have an invoice for them?
B: Yes, I do. Here you are.

---

customs declaration 報關單　　declare〔dɪˈklɛr〕*v.* 報關；申報

2

A： 請讓我看一下您的護照。

B： 在這兒。

A： 你打算待多久？

B： 兩個星期。

A： 你來的目的是什麼？

B： 我是來商務旅行的。

A： 知道了。那麼你打算住那裏呢？

B： 希爾頓飯店。

A： 很好。祝您在美國一切愉快。

3

A： 請讓我看一下您的申報單。

B： 在這兒。

A： 有什麼東西要申報的嗎？

B： 沒有，我帶的都是些個人用品。

A： 你介意打開行李箱嗎？

B： 一點也不。

A： 這包裹裏是什麼東西？

B： 一些生意上的樣本。

A： 有發票嗎？

B： 有，在這裏。

---

invoice 〔'ɪnvɔɪs〕 *n.* 發票

4

A： I couldn't claim my baggage.

B： Will you show us your baggage claim tag?

A： Yes. It's Flight 602 from Taipei.

B： All of the baggage from that flight has been cleared.

A： What should I do now?

B： Look at these samples and tell us the color, type and characteristics of your suitcase.

A： The type is this and the color is brown.

B： Okay. As soon as we find the suitcase we'll deliver it to your hotel.

SUPPLEMENTARY DIALOGS ———

A： Do you have anything to declare?

B： No. I have nothing to declare.

A： Do you have any tobacco products?

B： I have six cartons of cigarettes, but just for myself.

A： May I have your vaccination certificate?

B： Yes, sir. Here you are.

A： Do you have more than $5,000 in monetary instruments?

B： No. I have only $1,000 in T.C., and $300 in cash.

---

claim 〔klem〕 *v.* 認領

4

A： 我的行李不能領了。（行李丟了。）

B： 能讓我們看看你行李的認領標籤嗎？

A： 可以。是從台北來的六〇二號班機。

B： 那架飛機上所有的行李，都已經清光了。

A： 那麼，我現在應該怎麼辦？

B： 看看這些樣本，然後告訴我們你行李箱的顏色、式樣和特徵。

A： 式樣是這一型，顏色是棕色的。

B： 好的，我們一發現這個行李箱，會馬上送到您的旅館。

補充會話 ─────────────────

A： 你有沒有東西要申報？

B： 沒有。我沒有東西要申報。

A： 你帶了煙草製品嗎？

B： 我帶了六盒香煙，不過是自己要抽的。

A： 能讓我看看你的檢疫證明嗎？

B： 好的，先生。在這兒。

A： 你有沒有帶超過美金五千塊的貨幣證券？

B： 沒有。我只帶了一千美金的旅行支票和三百塊現金。

---

vaccination certificate 檢疫證明書

monetary instrument 貨幣證券

BUSINESS ADVICE

在機場辦理入境,依序要通過**檢疫官**(*quarantine officer*)、**移民局官員**(*immigration officer*)、**海關官員**(*customs inspector*)。當接受入境官員、海關官員問話的時候,最好能整句回答,在" Yes "和" No "之後,記得加上" Sir "。

◎ 入境通關步驟

1. 一開始移民局官員會鄭重地問:

May I see your passport?
(請讓我看一下您的護照好嗎?)

你應用整句回答,別忘了尊稱對方一句" Sir "。如:

Yes, Sir. Here's my passport and the arrival card.
(好的,長官。這是我的護照和入境卡。)

2. 移民局官員通常會提出一些基本問題,如:

May I have your disembarkation card, please?
(請讓我看一下您的登岸證明,好嗎?)

What's your purpose of visit?
(你這趟旅行的目的是什麼?)

How long do you intend to stay?
(你打算待多久?)

3. 移民局官員會登錄護照期限,並蓋章核可放行。入境審查結束

後，先在 ' baggage claim area ' 取回行李，然後到海關。

4. 在海關完稅時，官員會根據你的報關單，核對所攜帶的物品，提出質疑：

Do you have anything to declare ?
（你有什麼東西要申報嗎？）

Do you have any tobacco, liquor or perfume ?
（你有攜帶煙酒或香水嗎？）

Would you open this bag ?
（你可以打開這個袋子嗎？）

What's in this package ?
（這包裹裏是什麼？）

Is this for your own use ?
（這是自用的嗎？）

5. 萬一行李遺失，可至 " Lost and Found "（失物招領處），告訴櫃台人員說：

I can't find my suitcase.
（我找不到我的皮箱。）

I am afraid my baggage is lost.
（恐怕我的行李丢了。）

My baggage hasn't arrived here.
（我的行李還沒到。）

申報行李遺失時，記得出示行李保管證（claim tag），確定遺失後，則填妥 " Property Irregularity "，把失物特徵、自己姓名、住址記在上面。

Lesson 24

Using Public Transportation

MODEL DIALOGS ———————————

1

A : Where to, sir?

B : The Hilton, please.

A : Yes, sir.

B : How much to the Hilton?

A : From here... about $20.

B : All right. Let's go.

A : Here we are. $18.25 *on the meter*.

B : Here. *Keep the change*.

---

on the meter 照跳表算　　*keep the change* 不用找；保留零錢

第二十四課

使用大眾運輸工具

對話範例 ————————————

1

A：先生，到那裏？

B：請到希爾頓。

A：是的，先生。

B：到希爾頓要多少錢？

A：從這裏……大概要二十塊美金。

B：好的。開車吧！

A：到了。照表算，十八塊二毛五分。

B：給你，不用找了。

2

A: Take me to the airport, please.

B: Sure. *Get in*.

A: How long will it take?

B: We can make it in 15 minutes. It depends on the traffic.

A: Driver! Please hurry. I'*m pressed for* time.

B: All right, sir. Here we are.

A: How much do *I owe you*?

B: It comes to $28, sir.

A: I only have a $50 bill. Can you break it?

3

A: Is this the bus going to the Hilton Hotel?

B: Yeah. *Get on*.

A: *What's the fare*?

B: It's 50 cents.

A: (*Putting the fare into the fare box*) Please let me off when I get there.

A: Sure. Anyway it's five stops after this one.

B: I see.

---

get in 上車（搭乘汽車用 *get in*）　　traffic〔ˋtræfɪk〕*n.* 交通情況
be pressed for time 時間緊迫

2

A: 請載我到機場。

B: 沒問題。上車。

A: 要多久才會到?

B: 我們可以在十五分鐘以內趕到,要視交通情況而定。

A: 司機,請開快一點。我時間緊迫。

B: 沒問題,先生。我們到了。

A: 我應給你多少錢?

B: 二十八塊,先生。

A: 我只有五十元的整鈔。你能找開嗎?

3

A: 這輛公車到希爾頓飯店嗎?

B: 到,上車。

A: 車費多少?

B: 五十分。

A: (把錢放進車費箱) 到的時候,請讓我下車。

B: 當然。反正再過五站就到了。

A: 知道了。

I owe you 我應給你;我欠你   *get on* 上車 (搭乘公車用 *get on*)
fare〔fɛr〕*n.* 車費

4

A: I'd like to rent a car.

B: What kind of car would you like?

A: A *compact car*, please.

B: I see. May I see your driver's license, please?

A: Sure. What's the rate?

B: $35 a day and 20 cents a mile. You pay for the gasoline.

A: Is insurance covered?

B: Yes, it is. How long will you need it?

A: For 3 days.

SUPPLEMENTARY DIALOGS ———

A: Take me to this address, please.

B: Yes, sir. Get in.

A: Can you take me downtown?

B: OK.

A: Let me off here, please.

B: All right, sir.

A: I want to return this car.

B: Yes, sir. Could I see your contract?

---

compact car 小型車

4

A： 我想租車。

B： 喜歡哪一型的車？

A： 請給我小型車。

B： 知道了。我能看一下您的駕照嗎？

A： 當然了。車的租金怎麼算？

B： 一天美金三十五元，一哩二十分。油錢自付。

A： 費用包含保險費嗎？

B： 對。你需要租多久？

A： 三天。

補充會話────────────────────

A： 請載我到這個住址。

B： 好的，先生。上車！

A： 能載我到城裏去嗎？

B： 好的。

A： 請讓我在這裏下車。

B： 好的，先生。

A： 我要還車。

B： 好的，先生。能讓我看一下您的契約嗎？

BUSINESS ADVICE

在美國，計程車（cab）多半是黃色或橘色。要說出目的地時，可以說：

Would you go to the Hilton ?

The Hilton, please.
（請到希爾頓飯店。）

如果在大城市（如：紐約），而您的目的地是機場，那麼要說明機場名稱及位置：

Would you take me to the Kennedy Airport ?
（請載我到甘迺迪機場。）

Take me to 230 North Michigan Avenue, please.
（請載我到北密西根大道二百三十號。）

◈ **Tip! Tip!小費怎麼算？**

國外下車時，一定要給司機小費（tip）。

車資少於美金一塊半，小費給個五毛就不錯了。

車資在一塊半以上，大約給車費的10～15％，就可以了。

加載大皮箱，每個加收五毛錢。拿零錢當小費時，可以說：

Just keep the change.
（不用找零了。）

在美 國旅行，尤其是商務出差，最好租車，因為在美國，沒有車就好像沒有脚，行動實在不便。有許多著名的租車公司，如Hertz，Avis，National 等等，都在機場設有事務所。租車時，最好人車均保險，萬一出車禍，善後處理可以全交給租車公司處理。

租車方式可分以下三種，儘可能在約定日期內還車：

1. daily rates（按天計價）

2. weekly rates（按週計價）

3. monthly rates（按月計價）

除了 以上費用，隨公司不同，收費標準也不一樣，一般週末（週五下午至星期一早上）租車，要多加幾成費用，叫 " *weekend rates* "，通常是基本費外，再加一哩的駕駛費、稅金和保險費等。

Lesson 25

Checking into a Hotel

MODEL DIALOGS ————————

1

A : (*On the phone*) Reservations. May I help you?

B : Would you book a single room for two nights for me?

A : Certainly. When do you plan to stay with us?

B : From 15th to 17th of this month.

A : Yes, sir. May I have your name, please?

B : Tony Lee. T-O-N-Y L-E-E.

A : All right, sir. What time will you be arriving?

B : I'll probably check in at about 4 p.m..

A : I see. We'll keep your reservation until 6 o'clock.

B : Would you send me the confirmation by telex?

第二十五課

投宿旅館

對話範例————————————

1

A：（電話中）訂房部。我能替你效勞嗎？

B：能替我訂間單人房嗎？我要住兩晚。

A：當然可以。你打算什麼時候來？

B：這個月的十五號到十七號。

A：好的，先生。請問大名？

B：李東尼。

A：好的，先生。您什麼時候會到呢？

B：我可能會在下午四點左右到。

A：好的。我會把您的預約保留到六點。

B：你能用商務電報，再跟我確定一次嗎？

2

A: May I help you?

B: Yes. I have a reservation for tonight. My name is Tony Lee.

A: One moment, please. Yes, we have a room for you.

B: What's your check-out time?

A: It's one o'clock, sir. Would you *fill out* this registration card, please?

B: OK. Here you are.

A: Thank you. I'll get a bellboy to take you to your room.

3

A: I'd like a single for three nights. Do you have one available?

B: Yes, we do. Room 602.

A: *What's the room charge*?

B: Seventy dollars a night, including tax. How would you like to pay?

A: Card, please. May I take a look?

B: Here's your room. I hope it's all right.

A: Just fine, *I'll take it*. This is for you.

---

check-out 退房　　*fill out* 填寫

registration card 投宿登記卡　　bellboy〔'bɛl,bɔɪ〕*n.* 服務生

2

A：我能替你效勞嗎？

B：是的，我今晚定了個房間。我的名字是李東尼。

A：請稍待一會兒。我們替你留了間房。

B：你們退房的時間是幾點？

A：一點鐘。請填好這張登記卡。

B：好了，給你。

A：謝謝。我會找個服務生帶你到房間去。

3

A：我要一間單人房，住三晚。你有空房間嗎？

B：有，六○二號房。

A：房錢是多少？

B：一晚七十塊，含稅。你想怎麼付？

A：用信用卡。我能看一下房間嗎？

B：這是你的房間。希望你滿意，

A：還不錯，我決定住下來。這是給你的小費。

---

a single for three nights 單人房住三晚

I'll take it. 我決定租下它。

4

A: May I have your name, sir?

B: Tony Lee.

A: Just a moment, please. I'm sorry, but we don't have your reservation.

B: But it was confirmed last week. Here is the confirmation slip.

A: Oh, sorry, sir. Your reservation seems to be omitted.

B: Make another arrangement for me, please.

A: Yes, sir.

SUPPLEMENTARY DIALOGS ──

A: May I help you?

B: Yes. I'd like to check in, please.

A: How much do you charge for that room?

B: That's $80 a night, including tax.

A: I'm sorry, but *we're all booked up for tonight*.

B: Would you recommend another hotel? Around this hotel.

A: Your room is 305, sir.

B: I don't like it. A higher floor, please.

---

confirmation slip 預約確定書

4

A： 先生，請問大名？

B： 李東尼。

A： 請稍等一會兒。……抱歉，我們找不到你的預約。

B： 可是上禮拜才確定過的。這是預約確定書。

A： 先生，抱歉。你的預約好像漏掉了。

B： 請替我重新安排。

A： 是的，先生。

補充會話 ─────────────

A： 我能替你效勞嗎？

B： 是的。我想住宿。

A： 這間房間費用多少？

B： 一晚美金八十塊，含稅。

A： 抱歉，今晚已經客滿了。

B： 你願意介紹另一家旅館嗎？要在這附近的。

A： 先生，您住三〇五號房。

B： 我不喜歡。請換較高層的房間。

BUSINESS ADVICE

事先就已決定的旅行，出國前，一定先要預約好旅館，預約好了，儘可能要求旅館方面能將**預約確定書**（*confirmation slip*）郵寄過來，在出國時務必攜帶。旅館當然是選在交通便利，離工作場所較近的地方。能住一流旅館的話，會有更多的方便及好處。

美國旅遊協會（*American Hotel Association Directory Corporation*）所發行的 '*Hotel Red Book*'（旅館紅皮書），書中收錄了美國旅館名稱、電話號碼,還告訴您該旅館是屬於*American Plan*（**住宿包括餐費**），還是屬於*European Plan*（**餐費另計**）。

🔘 Check-in登記投宿

到旅館登記投宿（check-in）的時候,要向櫃台（Front Desk）出示**預約確定書**（*confirmation slip*），並說：

My name is Henry Smith. I have a reservation for tonight and tomorrow.
（我是約翰・史密斯。我訂了個房間，住今、明兩天。）

I have a reservation for a single room for tonight.
（今晚我訂了個單人房。）

預約確定後，則填具**投宿登記卡**(*registration card*)。

萬一，住宿費及房間種類，與所預約不符時，可以說：

I need the same accommo-
dations as stated in confirmation. Please make the ar-
rangements for me.

（我需要和預約確定時一樣的
食宿供給，請替我安排。）

預約結束後，bellman 或 bellboy（服務生）會從Front Desk（櫃台），取得鑰匙，提行李帶你到房間。bellman 到房間後，會檢查浴室蓮蓬頭是否完好，並調節室內溫度，把一切都檢查過後，bellman 才把鑰匙交給你。帶路和提行李的小費各為美金五毛。

● Check-out退房結帳

退 房結賬叫 " check-out ，" check-out "的時間各家旅館不一，超過規定時間，可能要多加一天住宿費。為了避免花宽枉錢，最好在 check-in 的時候，就問清楚，如：

Tell me the check-out time, please.
（請告訴我退房的時間。）

What's the check-out time?
（退房的時間是什麼時候？）

Lesson 26

Staying at a Hotel

MODEL DIALOGS ─────────

1

A : May I help you, sir?

B : Yes. I'*m supposed to* meet my client in the lobby. Could you page Mr. Kane, please?

A : All right, sir. Your name, please.

B : I'm Tony Lee.

A : Where would you like him to come?

B : To the front desk.

A : Just a moment, please. I'll *make the announcement* right away.

────────────

be supposed to 應該 (= *be expected to*)
client 〔'klaɪənt〕 *n.* 客戶

第二十六課

住在旅館

對話範例

1

A: 我能替你效勞嗎？

B: 可以。我應該和客戶在樓下大廳碰頭。能請你廣播一下肯恩先生嗎？

A: 先生，沒問題。請告訴我你的名字。

B: 我是李東尼。

A: 你要他到哪裏去？

B: 到前面櫃台去。

A: 請稍待一會兒。我馬上廣播。

---

page〔pedʒ〕*vt*.（在旅館中）廣播（喊名尋找某人）

announcement〔əˈnaʊnsmənt〕*n*. 廣播

2

A： (*On the phone*) Room Service. May I help you?

B： This is Mr. Lee in Room 803. I'd like to order a ham sandwich and a cup of coffee.

A： Thank you very much. It'll take about 15 minutes.

B： (*Someone knocks*) Come in.

C： I'm sorry for the delay, sir.

B： That's all right. Would you put it on this table.

C： Yes, sir.... Would you sign this chit, please?

B： OK.... And this is for you.

3

A： (*On the phone*) Operator. May I help you?

B： This is Mr. Lee in Room 803. I'd like *a wake-up call* in the morning.

A： Certainly. What time, sir?

B： Please call me at 6.

A： I see. We'll call you at 6 o'clock tomorrow morning.

B： Thank you very much. Good night!

---

chit 〔tʃɪt〕 *n.* 小型掛帳之單據

2

A：（電話中）房間服務部。我能替你效勞嗎？

B：我是八〇三號房的李先生。我想叫客火腿三明治和一杯咖啡。

A：非常感謝。這大概要花十五分鐘。

B：（有人敲門）請進。

C：先生，抱歉耽擱了一下。

B：沒關係。把東西放在桌上，好嗎？

C：是的，先生。麻煩請您簽一下收據，好嗎？

B：可以。這是給你的小費。

3

A：（電話中）接線生。我能替你效勞嗎？

B：我是八〇三號房的李先生。麻煩明天早上打電話叫醒我。

A：沒問題。什麼時候？

B：請六點叫我。

A：知道了。明天早上六點，我們會打電話叫你。

B：非常謝謝你。晚安。

---

a wake-up call 打電話叫人起床

4

A: ***Check out***, please.
B: Here's your bill, sir.
A: Thanks. I'll pay by American Express.
B: I see.... Would you please sign this?
A: Sure. Here you are.
B: This is your receipt, sir.
A: Thank you. And would you store my baggage until four o'clock?
B: Certainly, sir.

SUPPLEMENTARY DIALOGS————

A: ***Safe-deposit box***, please.
B: Yes, sir. Please put your articles in this box. And sign here, please.

A: Can I stay in my room till 3:00 p.m.?
B: You sure can. But there will be an additional 50% room charge.

A: I'd like to stay one more night.
B: Yes, sir.

A: Please have my bill ready, because I'd like to check out in about 30 minutes.
B: Very good, sir.

---

bill〔bɪl〕*n.* 帳單   receipt〔rɪˈsit〕*n.* 收據

4

A： 請結帳。

B： 先生，這裏是您的帳單。

A： 謝謝。我要用美國運通信用卡付帳。

B： 好的。請簽一下這個。

A： 沒問題。簽好了，給你。

B： 先生，這是您的收據。

A： 謝謝。您願意替我保管行李到下午四點嗎？

B： 當然可以。

補充會話───────────────

A： 我要開保險箱。

B： 好的，先生。請把您的東西放在箱子裏，然後在這裏簽名。

A： 我可以在房間裏待到三點鐘嗎？

B： 當然可以。不過要加付一半的房錢。

A： 我想多待一晚。

B： 好的，先生。

A： 請把我的帳結清，因為我要在三十分鐘以內退房。

B： 沒問題，先生。

---

safe-deposit box 保險箱

BUSINESS ADVICE

在旅館房間裏訂餐飲，如果要 room service 在半小時至一小時間送到，約要多收 10％左右的服務費，送餐點來的服務生，也要多給個 10％～15％的小費（tip），因此比出去吃要來得貴。要訂早餐，必須在前一天就預定好，一般都是在飲食送來時，先簽個名，退房時再一起付就行了。

整理寢具的服務生，每天給個 25～50 分小費，如果早上很早就退房，碰不到服務生的話，可以將小費放在床上、床邊或桌上。

有要事要早起，可要求旅館打 " wake-up call "，又叫 " morning call "（叫人起床的電話）較爲妥當。如：

I'd like to have a wake-up call at 7 tomorrow morning.
（我希望櫃台，明天早上七點，
打電話叫我起床。）

Check-out 之前，約一個半小時，就要先給 bellman 或 porter（搬行李的服務生）打電話，表示要 check out，請他們幫忙將行李運到門口。

雖然已經退房了，在搭機前還有時間，想外出採購或觀光的話，可向櫃台要求把行李寄放在 Baggage Rome（行李間）保管。為了方便客人，一般旅館都會答應這個要求，如果給 porter 一些小費的話，拿回行李時，會更方便。

除了上述的服務人員外，旅館裏還有：

doorman（門房）：在旅館門口，負責幫忙開門，調度計程車。

bell captain（服務員領班）：是 bellman 的監督，負責出售各種
　　　　　　　　　　　　種表演、音樂會的入場卷。

assistant manager（襄理）：負責解決顧客的不便，介紹旅館，
　　　　　　　　　　　　處理意外等工作，小費視情況，由美金二至十
　　　　　　　　　　　　元不等。

cashier（帳房）：負責收一切費用，如：住宿費及餐費等。

Lesson 27

A Business Call

MODEL DIALOGS —————————

1

A: May I help you?

B: Yes. I have an 11 o'clock appointment with Mr. Miles.

A: May I have your name, sir?

B: I'm Bill Chao of United Microelectronics Corp..

A: Oh, yes. Mr. Miles is expecting you. Just a moment. I'll tell him you're here.

B: Thank you.

A: Mr. Miles will see you now. Please go in.

B: Thank you.

第二十七課

商業電話

對話範例──────────────

1

A: 我能替你效勞嗎?

B: 我十一點和麥爾斯先生有約。

A: 請問大名?

B: 我是聯華電子的趙比利。

A: 喔,對,麥爾斯先生正在等你。請稍待一會兒。我會告訴他你已經來了。

B: 謝謝你。

A: 麥爾斯先生現在可以見你。請進。

B: 謝謝。

2

A：I'm here to see Mr. Brown.

B：Do you have an appointment with him this morning?

A：Not exactly.　I phoned him I'd try to come today.

B：I'm sorry, but he has a visitor right now.

A：Will it take long?

B：Could you wait one moment?

A：Sure.

B：He asks that you wait for about five minutes, sir.

3

A：Welcome to Harper Corporation.　Please have a seat.

B：Thank you.　Mr. Parker suggested I contact you.
　　This is an introductory letter from him.

A：Oh, he called me.

B：He asked me to *give* his best *regards to* you.

A：That's very kind of you.

B：Not at all.

A：I hope I can be of some help.

---

contact〔'kɑntækt〕*v.* 連繫

introductory letter 介紹信（= *letter of introduction*）

2

A： 我來這裏見布朗先生。

B： 你今天早上跟他約好了嗎？

A： 不盡然。我打電話告訴他，今天我想辦法過來一趟。

B： 抱歉，現在他有訪客。

A： 要等很久嗎？

B： 你能等一會兒嗎？

A： 當然。

B： 先生，他請你等五分鐘左右。

3

A： 歡迎到哈潑公司。請坐。

B： 謝謝。派克先生建議我跟你連繫。這是他的介紹信。

A： 喔，他打過電話給我。

B： 他要我向你致上最誠摯的問候。

A： 你真好。

B： 不必客氣。

A： 希望我能幫上忙。

---

regards 〔rɪˈgɑrdz〕 *n.pl.* 問候
give regards to sb. 向某人問候

4

A: Have you met Miss Smith, my secretary?

B: No, I haven't.

A: Miss Smith, this is Mr. Chao. He's with United Microelectronics Corp..

C: How do you do? I'm Jane Smith. Glad to meet you.

B: How do you do, Miss Smith? Glad to meet you, too.

C: Just call me Jane. I've heard a lot about you.

B: I hope it's not all bad.

SUPPLEMENTARY DIALOGS ——

A: Do you have an appointment?

B: No, but I have a letter of introduction. Will you hand this to him?

A: What has brought you to the States this time?

B: It's a sales promotion trip for our new line.

A: I brought along this for you.

B: Oh, is it for me? You really shouldn't have.

A: Did you have any difficulty finding the office?

B: No, I didn't. The simple map you mailed helped me a lot.

---

new line 新產品

4

A： 你見過我的秘書，史密斯小姐嗎？

B： 沒見過。

A： 史密斯小姐，這是趙先生。他服務於聯華電子。

C： 你好，我是珍‧史密斯。很高興認識你。

B： 你好，史密斯小姐。我也很高興認識你。

C： 叫我珍就行了。我聽過很多跟你有關的事。

B： 希望不全是壞事。

補充會話────────────

A： 你已經約好了嗎？

B： 沒有，不過我有封介紹信。你能把信交給他嗎？

A： 這次是什麼風把你吹到美國來的？

B： 是替我們新產品系列做巡迴促銷的。

A： 我帶這個給你。

B： 喔，給我的？你實在不應該如此破費。

A： 找到辦公室不難吧？

B： 不難。你寄給我的簡圖，幫了我很多忙。

BUSINESS ADVICE

如 果是經秘書介紹見面，寒喧過後，馬上進入主題是無妨的。

隨地方不同，從打招呼到開始談業務的時間，多少各不相同。以美國爲例，大都市（如：New York）的商人在互道姓名、公司名稱之後，就馬上進入主題，而越小的都市，商人進入主題的時間就越長。

● You-Attitude→替對方著想

商談中，常用" I "或" We "爲首的句子，會顯得太過自我中心，不如使用所謂的" You-Attitude "，即站在對方的立場，多替對方著想。譬如常提對方的姓名，會給對方親切、受重視的感覺。如：

Mr. Brown, it would be your interest to accept this contract.
（布朗先生，接受這份合約，會對你有利。）

萬 一，會談進行中，雙方突然無話可話，不妨藉機休息，換換話題，緩和氣氛。如：

Shall we have a break for coffee ?
（我們休息一下，喝杯咖啡，好嗎？）

How about knocking off for a while ?
（何不休息一下呢？）

Let's take a 10-minutes break, shall we ?
（我們休息十分鐘，好不好？）

● 會談時間

會談中，擅自決定是不可能，碰到這情況，可以說：

Let me have word with my boss.
（讓我跟老板商量一下。）

表示自己無權決定，可能會給人過
於謹慎的印象。如果想爭取時間，不妨說：

Please let me think it over.
（請讓我考慮一下。）

Let me sleep on it.
（讓我斟酌一下。）

商談費時太久，是很失禮的，所以進行三十分鐘以後，最好先
問對方有沒有空，以免打擾過久。

● TIME IS UP.

如果覺得商談應該中止了，就應該明快地說：

Well, I think I must be going now.
（好吧，我想我得走了。）

如果想進一步會談，就先約定下次會面時間，也可使對方留下
好印象。

商談結束，離開辦公室前，別忘了留下一句：

It was a very nice meeting.
（這是次非常愉快的見面。）

讓整次會面有一個圓滿的結束。

Lesson 28

Making an International Call

MODEL DIALOGS————————

1

A: (*On the phone*) Hello. I'd like to call Taiwan.

B: One moment, please. I'll get an overseas operator for you.

A: Thank you.

C: This is the overseas operator. May I help you?

A: Yes; I'd like to call to Taipei. The number is 769 — 1611.

C: Is this a *person-to-person* or *station-to-station* call?

A: I want to make a person-to-person call to Mr. Park.

---

person-to-person call 叫人電話

第二十八課

打國際電話

對話範例

1

A： （電話中）喂，替我接台灣。

B： 請稍待。我替你找國際接線生。

A： 謝謝你。

C： 這裏是國際台。能替你效勞嗎？

A： 是的，請接台北，電話號碼是 769 — 1611 。

C： 叫人還是叫號？

A： 叫人，我要找派克先生。

---

station-to-station call 叫號電話

2

A : (*On the phone*) What number are you calling?

B : Taipei 575 — 3531. I'd like to make a call to Mr. Andy Park.

A : How do you spell his name?

B : A—N—D—Y　P—A—R—K.

A : I see.

B : How long will it take to get through to Taipei?

A : About two minutes, sir.

B : ***What's the toll***?

3

A : (*On the phone*) Overseas Operator. May I help you?

B : I'd like to call to Taipei. This is a collect call.

A : What number do you wish to call?

B : 782 — 3080.

A : Who would you wish to talk to?

B : I'll talk to anyone. It's my office.

A : What is the number you're calling from?

B : I'm calling from Chicago, (312) 674 — 8891.

A : Thank you. I'll call you back when your party is on the line.

---

toll 〔 tol 〕 *n.* 電話費

2

A： （電話中）你要撥幾號？

B： 台北575－3531。我要打給安廸·派克先生。

A： 他的名字怎麼拼？

B： A－N－D－Y　P－A－R－K。

A： 知道了。

B： 要花多久時間，才能跟台北接通？

A： 先生，大約要兩分鐘。

B： 電話費多少？

3

A： （電話中）國際接線生。我能替你效勞嗎？

B： 我要打電話到台北，對方付費。

A： 電話號碼幾號？

B： 782－3080。

A： 要跟誰通話呢？

B： 任何人都可以。那是我辦公室。

A： 你打過來的電話，號碼是幾號？

B： 我從芝加哥打來的，電話是（312）674－8891。

A： 謝謝。等你那邊接通了，我會回你電話。

---

collect call 對方付費電話　　*on the line* 電話接通了

4

A: (*On the phone*) Operator. May I help you?
B: Yes, I'd like to place *a station call* to New York.
The number is (212) 564 — 6095.
A: Who do you want to speak to?
B: Mr. John Smith. And this is Tony Lee, Room 803.
A: How would you like it billed, sir?
B: Bill it to my room, please.
A: Please hang up and wait till we call you back.

SUPPLEMENTARY DIALOGS ——

A: May I speak to Mr. Watson in the Export Department?
B: Hold on a minute, I'll connect you.

A: This is Atlantic Company. May I help you?
B: Yes. May I have Ext. 2147?

A: Can I make *a direct-dial call* to Korea from my room?
B: Yes, you can. Please dial 0—00—81. Then the area
code and the number in Korea.

A: Then connection is bad and I can't hear well. Will
you put me through again?
B: I'm awfully sorry for the trouble. I'll connect you
again.

---

direct-dial call 直接撥號電話
Ext. = extension 〔ɪkˈstɛnʃən〕 *n.* 分機（號碼）

4

A： （電話中）接線生。我能替你效勞嗎？

B： 是的，我想打個叫號的電話到紐約。電話號碼是（212）564 — 6059。

A： 你要跟誰說話呢？

B： 約翰·史密斯先生。我是李東尼，住八○三號房。

A： 先生，您打算怎麼付帳呢？

B： 請記在我帳上。

A： 請掛電話，等我們回你電話。

補充會話 ━━━━━━━━━━━━━━━

A： 請找出口部的華森先生。

B： 請稍待一會兒，我來替你接通。

A： 大西洋公司。我能替你效勞嗎？

B： 請接分機 2147。

A： 我能從房間打直撥電話到韓國嗎？

B： 可以。請撥 0 — 00 — 81。然後再撥韓國的區域號碼和電話號碼，就行了。

A： 線路很糟，我聽不清楚。你能再打一次嗎？

B： 給你惹麻煩，我真的很抱歉。我再打一次給你。

BUSINESS ADVICE

打 國際電話時，有下列幾種通話方式，可供選擇，應視本身及對方的情形決定。

1. 叫號（ *station-to-station call* / *station call* ）

告訴接線生對方的電話號碼，不管誰接，從開始到結束，都要算錢，不過比叫人的電話便宜。

2. 叫人（ *person-to-person call* / *personal call* ）

告訴接線生對方的電話號碼，並指明對象來接，計錢方式由所指定對象接到電話後，開始計費，每秒單價較高。

如果呼叫的對方，不是個人而是一個部門，也視為叫人電話。（如本課對話範例3）。打叫人電話可以說：

Operator, I want to make a person-to-person call to Boston. The name of the party I want to speak to is Mr. Brown.

（接線生，我要打一通叫人的電話到波士頓，我要找的人是布朗先生。）

3. 對方付費（ *collect call* ）

是由接電話的一方付費，所以接線生要先徵得對方同意，才能
接通。接線生會這麼問：

This is the United States calling. You have a collect
call from Mr. Smith in San Francisco. Will you accept
the charges？

（這是美國打來的電話。有位史密斯先生從舊金山，打對方付
費的電話給你。你願意付費嗎？）

表示願意接，可以說：

Yes, I will. Will you let me know the time and the
charges after the call？

（對，我會付錢。電話結束後，請讓我知道時間和價錢。）

4. 信用卡付費（ *credit card call* ）

利用國際電信局開發的 credit card 付費，是事後付款，對旅
行者十分方便。也可以不經交換總機，直接撥號，目前我國已
開放這項服務。

Lesson 29

Making Airline Travel Arrangements

MODEL DIALOGS —————————

1

A : (*On the phone*) Pan Am Reservations. May I help you?

B : I want to fly to L.A. the day after tomorrow. Can I reserve a seat?

A : Is this economy or first class?

B : Economy.

A : We have Flight 203 leaving at 3:20, arriving at 4.

B : That's perfect. Please book me on that flight.

A : Yes, sir. May I have your name and telephone number?

---

economy class 經濟客艙

第二十九課

安排航空旅行

對話範例 ────────

1

A： （電話中）泛美航空訂位處。我能替你效勞嗎？

B： 後天我要搭機飛往洛杉磯。可以給我預定個座位嗎？

A： 要經濟艙還是頭等艙？

B： 經濟艙。

A： 我們二〇三號班機在三點二十分起飛，四點到達。

B： 太好了。請替我訂這班機。

A： 好的，先生。請留下姓名及電話號碼。

────────

first class 頭等艙

2

A： (*On the phone*) Parker Travel Agency.

B： Would you tell me if there's a morning flight from New York to San Francisco on March 20?

A： There's a **non-stop flight** leaving from Kennedy Airport at 7:30.

B： I won't be able to get up that early.

A： Then, Universal Flight 608 leaves at 10:00, but it has an hour's layover in Chicago.

B： What time does it arrive in San Francisco?

A： It's 12:15. Will that be satisfactory?

B： Yes, that's fine.

3

A： (*On the phone*) I'm calling to **confirm my reservation**?

B： Your name and the flight number, please.

A： My name is Tony Lee. The flight number is 504 on the 8th of this month from New York to Chicago.

B： Just a moment, please... OK, I've confirmed your reservation.

A： Thank you very much for your help.

B： You're very welcome. Is there anything else I can help you with?

2

A：（電話中）派克旅行社。

B：你能告訴我，三月二十號早上，有飛機飛紐約到舊金山嗎？

A：七點半有班直飛班機從甘迺迪機場出發。

B：那麼早我起不來。

A：那麼，環球六〇八號班機十點起飛，但中途會在芝加哥停留一小時。

B：什麼時候到舊金山呢？

A：十二點十五分到。可以嗎？

B：可以。

3

A：（電話中）我打電話來確定機位的。

B：請告訴我名字和班機號碼。

A：我的名字是李東尼。搭乘班機是這個月八號，從紐約飛往芝加哥的五〇四號班機。

B：請稍待一會兒。……好了，我已經確定你的機位。

A：非常謝謝你的幫忙。

B：不客氣。其他還有什麼事，我能幫忙的嗎？

---

non-stop flight 直飛　　　layover〔ˈle,ovɚ〕n. 中途停留

4

A : Good morning, sir. Your ticket, please.

B : Flight 203 to San Francisco.

A : May I see your passport?

B : Yes. Here it is.

A : Smoking or non-smoking?

B : Smoking, please.

A : That'll be 11C. Any baggage, sir?

B : Yes, these two pieces and one carry-on.

A : Your flight will be boarding at Gate #32 at 6:20.

SUPPLEMENTARY DIALOGS ———

A : What's first class fare to New York?

B : The fare is $180.

A : Is the flight *on schedule*?

B : Yes, it's on time.

A : First class and economy class are both completely occupied.

B : Will you put me on the *waiting list*?

A : I'd like to change my routing.

B : May I have your name and flight number?

---

carry-on〔ˈkærɪˈɑn,-ɔn〕 *n.* 隨身攜帶行李

4

A： 早安 ，先生 。請讓我看一下您的機票 。
B： 二〇三號班機 ，往舊金山 。
A： 能讓我看看您的護照嗎 ？
B： 可以 ，在這裏 。
A： 吸煙區還是非吸煙區 ？
B： 請給我吸煙區的位子 。
A： 那就是 11C 。有沒有行李呢 ？
B： 有的 ，有兩件託運 ，一件隨身攜帶的 。
A： 您的飛機在六點二十分的時候 ，會停在三十二號機門 。

補充會話 ——————————————

A： 到紐約的頭等艙機位 ，多少錢 ？
B： 美金一百八十塊 。

A： 這班機會準時嗎 ？
B： 對 ，會準時 。

A： 頭等艙和經濟客艙都已經客滿了 。
B： 能不能把我列入補位呢 ？

A： 我想改變行程 。
B： 請告訴我大名和班機號碼 。

———————————————

waiting list 補位行列　　routing 〔′rutɪŋ〕 *n.* 行程

BUSINESS ADVICE

搭乘飛機出國，最方便的方法就是，請旅行社（Travel Agency）代辦手續。要訂機票時，要向該航空公司的訂位處（reservation desk），查詢公司名、電話號碼、出發時間、到達時間，等等。如：

Do you have a flight from New York to Boston on Jun. 10?
（請問六月十號有沒有，從紐約飛往波士頓的班機？）

I'd like to reserve two economy class seats on October 24.
（我想預約十月二十四號，兩個經濟客艙的機位。）

為了應付可能發生更動訂位的事，最好問清經手的辦事員（clerk）的姓名，還要記得確定機位（confirmation）。如：

I'd like to confirm my reservations. My name is Bruce Lee. I have a reservation on Flight No. 331 from New York to Hawaii on September 14.

（我想確定一下預約的機位。我的名字是希魯斯·李。我預約九月十四號，從紐約飛往夏威夷的三三一號班機。）

搭機前三天，必須再確定機位，否則預約會失效，機位便被取消。

◎ 變更行程

萬一，搭機日期變更，應該打電話通知航空公司：

I'd like to change my flight reservation.
（我想更改飛行班次。）

I'd like to change my reservation from an economy class to a first class.
（我想把機位從經濟艙改為頭等艙。）

如果機票已經買好了，可以帶機票到最近的航空公司(airline office)，要求變更機票，這就叫做 "*revalidate*"（重新確定機位）（= *reconfirm*）。

如果是在同一家公司，變更預約是免費的。如果換航空公司，換班機飛行路線，換目的地，因而費用有所不同的話，採多退少補的辦法。

Lesson 30

An Emergency

MODEL DIALOGS ────────────

1

A: (*On the phone*) Hello, this is David Wang. Your name was recommended to me by the American Consulate.

B: What can I do for you?

A: I am not feeling well. I'm visiting your city on business.

B: What exactly is bothering you?

A: I have a sharp pain in my stomach. Could I come to your office now?

B: I have an opening at 10:30 this morning. Will that be convenient?

A: That will be fine. Thank you.

第三十課

緊急情況

對話範例 —————————————————

1

A： （電話中）喂，我是王大衞。美國領事館向我推薦你。

B： 我能爲你做什麼呢？

A： 我覺得身體不舒服。我到你們城裏出差。

B： 到底是什麼問題呢？

A： 我的胃突然很痛。我現在可以到你辦公室來嗎？

B： 我今天早上十點半開始營業。那時你有空嗎？

A： 有空。謝謝你。

---

consulate 〔ˈkɑnsjəlɪt, ˈkɑnslɪt〕 *n.* 領事館

stomach 〔ˈstʌmək〕 *n.* 胃　　opening 〔ˈopənɪŋ, ˈopnɪŋ〕 *n.* 開始營業

2

A : What seems to be the problem?

B : I have a bad case of diarrhea.

A : Have you had anything unusual to eat in the past few days?

B : Not that I can think of.

A : It doesn't look like anything serious to me.

B : That's a relief. Can I continue my trip?

A : Sure. But try to get some rest. I'll just *write out a prescription* for you.

3

A : What can I do for you, sir?

B : Do you have something for a cold?

A : Any particular brand?

B : No, please suggest a good one. I'm not familiar with American brands.

A : This is the current number one brand in America.

B : All right. How often do I take it?

A : You should take this three times a day within 30 minutes after meals. I'll give you two day's worth.

---

diarrhea 〔͵daɪə′riə〕 *n.* 腹瀉

relief 〔rɪ′lif〕 *n.* (痛苦、困難、負擔等之) 解除；減輕

2

A: 問題可能出在那裏呢？

B: 我嚴重腹瀉。

A: 最近幾天，你有沒有吃過什麼不尋常的東西？

B: 我想沒有。

A: 看起來沒什麼嚴重的嘛。

B: 那我就放心了。我能繼續旅行嗎？

A: 當然。不過要多休息。我會開處方給你。

3

A: 先生，我能爲你做什麼？

B: 有沒有感冒藥？

A: 要什麼特別的牌子嗎？

B: 沒有，請介紹個好牌子。我對美國牌子不熟悉。

A: 這是現在美國最好的牌子。

B: 好吧。多久服用一次？

A: 你應該一天服用三次，飯後半小時內服用。我給你兩天份。

---

prescription〔prɪˈskrɪpʃən〕*n.* 處方

4

A: (*On the phone*) I'd like to report a burglary.

B: Where are you?

A: I'm staying at the Hilton Hotel, Room 803.

B: When did the theft occur?

A: Sometime this morning, I think. When I returned to my hotel room this afternoon, I found my camera missing.

B: Was anything else stolen?

A: No, I placed all my other valuables in the hotel safe.

B: We will be right over.

SUPPLEMENTARY DIALOGS ———

A: Operator, I need to see a doctor.

B: Right away? Is it serious, sir?

A: Do you have any insurance?

B: No. I'll pay in cash.

A: I accidentally broke my glasses. Could you make a new pair for me?

B: Do you have the prescription?

A: I'd like to report a theft. My camera was stolen.

B: When did it occur?

---

burglary〔ˈbɜɡlərɪ〕 *n.* 竊盜

4

A： （電話中）我要報案，是竊案。

B： 你在哪裏呢？

A： 我在希爾頓飯店，八〇三號房。

B： 竊案是何時發生的？

A： 我想是今天早上。我今天下午回到旅館房間時，發現照相機不見了。

B： 還有什麼東西被偷？

A： 沒有。我把所有貴重的東西都放在旅館保險箱裏。

B： 我們馬上過去。

補充會話

A： 接線生，我需要看醫生。

B： 馬上嗎？嚴重嗎，先生？

A： 你有保險嗎？

B： 沒有。我付現金。

A： 我不小心打破眼鏡。能替我配付新的嗎？

B： 有醫生指示嗎？

（註：配眼鏡前，要先至醫生那兒驗光，按醫生指示配鏡）

A： 我要報案，是竊案。我的照相機被偷了。

B： 什麼時候發生的？

---

valuables 〔ˊvæljuəblz〕 *n.pl.* 貴重物品

BUSINESS ADVICE

天有不測風雲，人有旦夕禍福，萬一在出差期間，在海外碰到疾病纏身或遭竊，交通意外，等意外災難時，建議採取以下的對策：

1. 身體不適

身體不適應立即就醫，可從電話簿上找到醫院名稱及電話，打電話預約後，直接去看病。歐美醫療費用是分開計算的，醫生只收診查和處方費用，藥品則持醫師處方，自行到藥局購買。感冒藥，腸胃藥等無處方，也能買得到。以下是身體不適，常用的話：

I feel very sick.
（我想吐。）

I think I have a fever.
（我覺得我發燒。）

I have a cold and a hacking cough.
（我感冒，乾咳。）

I have a headache and chills.
（我頭痛，受寒了。）

I have a sore throat and can't take any food down.
（我喉嚨痛，吃不下任何食物。）

I have a stomachache.
（我胃痛。）

I have a piercing pain in my chest.
（我胸口像撕裂一般疼痛。）

I have an earache and feel dizzy.
（我耳朵痛，覺得昏沉沉的。）

I have my elbow twisted.
（我的肘扭到了。）

I have a diarrhea.
（我拉肚子。）

2. 遭竊／遭劫

⇨ 身邊儘可能少帶錢，貴重物品或錢存在旅館保險箱（safe-deposit box）裏。

⇨ 少去黑暗，人跡罕至的地方。

⇨ 遇到暴徒，不可抵抗，聽從他一切要求，以保命爲第一要務。

3. 交通事故

⇨ 自己開車，出車禍可打電話通知警察或醫院，撥0號，報告總機，車禍的位置及情況亦可。

⇨ 車禍後，千萬不要說" I am sorry～"，否則等於是認錯，不只是警察調查時，會對自己不利，領保險公司賠償金，也會有所損失。

心得筆記欄

Editorial Staff

- **修編** / 陳怡平
- **英文撰稿**

  David Bell · Bruce S. Stewart

  Edward C. Yulo · John C. Didier

- **校訂**

  劉　毅·葉淑霞·陳怡平·陳威如·王慶銘

  王怡華·林順隆·許碧珍·林佩汀·陳瑠琍

- **校閱**

  Larry J. Marx · Lois M. Findler

  John H. Voelker · Keith Gaunt

- **封面設計** / 張鳳儀
- **插畫** / 林惠貞·王孝月
- **版面設計** / 張鳳儀·張端懿
- **版面構成** / 蘇淑玲
- **打字**

  黃淑貞·倪秀梅·蘇淑玲·吳秋香·徐湘君

||||||||||||| ● 學習出版公司門市部 ● |||||||||||||||||

台北地區：台北市許昌街 10 號 2 樓 TEL：(02)2331-4060・2331-9209
台中地區：台中市綠川東街 32 號 8 樓 23 室
　　　　　TEL：(04)223-2838

|||||||||||||||||||||||||||||||||||||||||||||||||

客戶接待英文

修　　編 / 陳怡平
發 行 所 / 學習出版有限公司　　　　☎ (02) 2704-5525
郵 撥 帳 號 / 0512727-2 學習出版社帳戶
登 記 證 / 局版台業 2179 號
印 刷 所 / 裕強彩色印刷有限公司
台 北 門 市 / 台北市許昌街 10 號 2 F　　☎ (02) 2331-4060・2331-9209
台 中 門 市 / 台中市綠川東街 32 號 8 F 23 室　　☎ (04) 223-2838
台灣總經銷 / 紅螞蟻圖書有限公司　　☎ (02) 2799-9490・2657-0132
美國總經銷 / Evergreen Book Store　　☎ (818) 2813622

售價：新台幣一百八十元正
2001 年 1 月 1 日一版七刷